I'M A CATCH...
AREN'T I?

Lorraine Cambria

Published in the United States by Cambria Publishing, LLC.

ISBN-13: 978-1532980350
ISBN-10: 1532980353

Book design by David Verchick
Cover design by David Verchick

I'M A CATCH...
AREN'T I?

Lorraine Cambria

Cambria Publishing, LLC

This one's for all the single ladies...

and the trifecta of perfection in my life:
Mom, Dad, and Christina

CONTENTS

Introduction

THERE ARE A LOT OF UNANSWERED QUESTIONS in my life right now. *Is there a higher being? What's the real reason that Zayn left One Direction? Why the HELL did Josh and Andi, from* The Bachelorette, *break up?* As frustratingly mysterious as these questions are, perhaps the question that bothers me the most is related to my love life: *why doesn't anything ever seem to work out?*

It is an inquiry that's plagued me for years. I was in kindergarten when I first started to become entangled in matters of love and lust. My cubby was adjacent to another cubby that belonged to a fine five-year-old fellow named Ken. An inexplicable feeling overcame me the moment Ken and I first locked eyes whilst trying to shove all of our crap into those little makeshift wooden closets. Suddenly, I wanted to spend every minute of every school day at Ken's side. Unfortunately for me, Ken wouldn't give me the time of day. Literally. During a learning exercise to tell time, Ken turned his back to me when I asked him a pointed question. It was my first taste of the bitter, stupid fruit of rejection.

I wish I could say that it got better after kindergarten – that the bitter fruit of rejection ripened into a sweeter, healthier crop of romantic success squash. It would be nice if I could talk about a time when everything worked out between me and a guy I liked. I would love to report that there was even *just one* experience with *one* guy that ended well. Ultimately, things between him and me ended, but it was only because we loved each other too much or because he was an astronaut who was flying to space and is still in space right now where he will remain for the next 500 years, exploring new planets and befriending aliens. But I can't truthfully say anything of that nature. That has never happened. Frankly, nothing has ever happened to get me even fifty feet within the area of that sort of relationship and its subsequent tragically beautiful ending.

Because I've never had a boyfriend.

There. I said it! I am 24 years old and I have never had a boyfriend. I've known guys, I've spoken to guys, I've flirted with guys (if I'm correctly interpreting flirting), I've kissed guys, I've dated guys – I don't mean to brag, but I've been on at least five, maybe even six, official dates. Actually, there have been quite a few times when I've come painfully close to having a boyfriend. But not close enough. Nothing has ever worked out well with a guy, particularly in the form of a happy, thriving, long-term relationship. Hell, nothing has ever worked out well enough to manifest in even a sweetly satisfying, official, short-term relationship.

Only in my imagination have I had a sweet but sexy, funny and smart, lovably protective boyfriend with an eight-pack of abdominal muscles. In this fantasy world, with this hypothetical beau of mine, I am constantly barraged with compliments on what a handsome and dynamic duo he and I make up. My friends dub us a perfect power couple, beautiful enough to rival even Brad and Angelina. Strangers on the street stop my boyfriend and me – not because they think we're famous or to ask us for directions, but because they want to take a photograph of us. They've never seen a love so pure, and they want physical proof that such a magnificent thing exists. My hypothetical love life is amazing. I have quite the boyfriend. He is beautiful. Our relationship is beautiful. But it is a beauty that does not translate to my real love life.

In real life, strangers on the street only stop me to ask for directions (or that one time, to tell me that they thought my One Direction backpack was stupid). The only power couple I've ever been a part of was with my dog – once – when I convinced him to eat a plain, organic carrot... no peanut butter or anything! But that broke up the next day when I tried again and he dramatically spit it out like he had just learned that it was carrot flavored poison.

In real life, along with unanswered questions, there are also a lot of "never's" surrounding me, thanks to my single, things-never-work-out status. Here is a sampling of some:

- I've never been able to use the words "my boyfriend" in a sentence and be talking about an actual person that exists in my life. Usually, when I'm referring to "my boyfriend" in a sentence, I am talking to an elderly person who doesn't know about One Direction. "You like coffee? That's so funny. *My boyfriend,* Harry Styles, he's very good at singing and he likes coffee, too!"

- I've never had a boyfriend to "act totally natural" with while my sister "unassumingly" takes pictures of us, resulting in a plethora of priceless "candid" photos that effortlessly capture the carefree yet passionate nature of our affection for one another.

- I've never cooked a boyfriend a dinner so delectable that he falls in love with me even more, providing proof that the way to a man's heart is indeed through his stomach.

- I've never had the opportunity to craft a boyfriend a homemade Valentine, which would be the perfect balance of corny and cool, expressing the depth of my feelings for him in an artistic and heartfelt way. My dad is the only man who's ever brought me a box of heart-shaped donuts on Valentine's Day – never a boyfriend.

- I've never had a boyfriend to surprise me on my birthday

with a gargantuan balloon bouquet and an impromptu pancake breakfast to celebrate the day I (his queen) was born.

- I've never known what it's like to spend Halloween with a boyfriend. Last year, I spent it hiding from trick-or-treaters, furtively leaving them old packages of instant hot chocolate on my doorstep because I ate all of the candy while I was by myself, becoming more emotional than I'd like to admit catching up on *Dancing With the Stars*.

- I've never taken a boyfriend to a Thanksgiving dinner for eating turkey and meeting my family. I've never had to hope that everyone would get along and NOT argue over politics or everyone's favorite season of *Friends*. So, I've never had the opportunity to comfort myself with the realization that, even if it all went south and Uncle Glenn and my boyfriend went head-to-head over season seven versus season nine, I wouldn't care because he would look so sexy in the dark grey sweater that I bought him.

- I've never had a boyfriend to take me ice-skating. I hate ice-skating. But is it so much to want the option of going ice-skating with a boyfriend? He would probably laugh at how terrible I am on the ice, and then try to help me, but I'd fall and take him down with me. We'd laugh some more and then kiss and he'd buy me a hot chocolate with extra whipped cream and baby marshmallows. Or something like that.

Sometimes it's all too easy to dwell on the "never's" in my life and wonder why they're "never's" instead of memories. I have had a lot of experiences with a lot of guys, but why have none of them provided any sort of security in the form of ice-skating together or celebrating Halloween as a couple? All I have to show for my past with guys is a lot of rockiness, uncertainty, and disappointment, which inevitably leads to the worst of it all: heartbreak. One might think that since there are no boyfriends to lose or to break up with, single ladies have it emotionally easy. Well, "one" who believes that: you are quite mistaken. Single ladies still endure deceptively devastating heartbreak. It is the heartbreak of disillusion. Every time I "say goodbye" to one of my "almost boy-friends" or "pre-relationships," I *am* breaking up with someone. I'm breaking up with a fantasy boyfriend — an idea I created in my mind to coincide with the real-life guy I've been talking to, or hanging out with, or crushing on. Since I'm not in a relationship with this guy, and it never gets officially serious, I am able to build these images and fantasies by way of my "he is practically perfect" goggles. Because he and I don't get as close as we would within a relationship, I don't know the guy as well as I think I do. Instead of actually having a relationship with him, I end up daydream-ing about what a relationship might be like with him — and, oh, what a sweet paradise of satisfaction. There are no limitations in a fantasy relationship, no expectations crushed or broken. When I envision "my guy" in a relationship with me in my mind, he is an amazing boyfriend who always does and says the most wonderful things. He smells really good and finds my passion for reality tele-vision endearing. We always have fun when we are together and he is a fantastic kisser. Sure, he has his "flaws," like he works too hard at his job or cares too much about the elderly. But he never picks his nose when I'm not looking, and he never flirts with other women. No. My fantasy boyfriend always uses a tissue and only has eyes for me. So, in a way, when the time comes, it's harder to let go. When I've finally realized that nothing is going to hap-pen with the current object of my affection, I become very sad and can't help but feel a sense of loss. I'm losing the possibility of sharing a great relationship with a wonderful boyfriend. But the fact is, sometimes I don't know the guy well enough to get a sense of what the relationship would actually be like. I don't know that it would be great and I'm not sure he'd be a wonderful boyfriend at all. Without the experience of a relationship, I don't and can't know if he has idiosyncrasies that would become troublesome long-term or how he would treat me as his girlfriend. It's harder for me to recognize his flaws and capitalize on them because, in most cases, I never got far enough with him to realize that he has any. We don't fight; he doesn't say mean things or reveal bad habits. He is fiercely protected by the ever-misleading "he is practically perfect" goggles. The fantasy is never tainted by reality.

It really is quite a confusing predicament. I am perpetually single, and yet, I still experience heartbreak. And I don't think I'm doing anything so horrifically wrong to justify my constant single status. By now, with my series of close encounters, I'd think at least one of them would've clicked; something should've stuck.

So why doesn't it ever work out?

It's a frustrating question. I wish I had a good answer. I think and think and think and think on it and try to gather some semblance of understanding, and yet − in the maddening search for answers − I remain an uninformed dummy in the dark, feeling pretty blue. The rumination inevitably leads me to think that something *is* wrong with me... that I'm some sort of un-dateable loser destined to end up alone surrounded by cat food, and no cats.

Every time I come to this conclusion, friends and family try to convince me otherwise.

"You're a catch," my Gram encourages in a strong and confident voice. She speaks with such enthusiasm that I almost believe her. She even postponed eating her cherry Danish to utter these words.

Am I though, Gram? Am I? Aren't catches, well, caught?

I don't know. Maybe Gram is right. When I'm in a more rational state of mind, I realize that all of the females whom I hold in the highest regard are in my same place. Then, I think a little more and realize that even the women whom I don't care as deeply for are in the same spot. Hell, women who are basically strangers to me but for us being "friends" on different social media sites are also going through the same thing. We are all in the same metaphorical boat, braving the tempestuous waters of dating together. That's when it dawns on me. Perhaps I'm not a lost cause – not just yet. Because it isn't just me. I'm not the only one consistently having the toxic and exhausting experiences of liking guys only to get let down by them, again and again. And again. The number of women out there in the world who find themselves all alone on Memorial Day Weekend, with no handsome lads to introduce as their boyfriends at pool parties, or wherever gals are supposed to go with their significant others on Memorial Day, is abysmal.

There are thousands of great girls – nay, amazing girls – who are the whole package, and yet, nothing ever seems to work out for them in love. I can personally vouch for about a dozen of them. All of my closest friends fall into this frustrating category. They are incredible and beautiful girls, but not one of them can say that things ever work out well when it comes to guys. My sister is gorgeous, smart, and kind. She loves good music. I mean really good, cool, music, too (no, I'm not referring to Fifth Harmony, but I do feel you, home girl who thought that's what I meant). She is ridiculously funny and has an ass that won't quit, something I remind her of probably more than she feels is necessary. But, amidst all her wonderfulness, a guy she really liked just recently disappointed her big-time. My best friend, Ann, is super pretty with a smile that lights up the world. She appreciates a romantic comedy just as much as a critically acclaimed independent film, and will happily sit through the typical superhero movie most guys drool over. She's creative, has a stunning positive energy, and kicks butt at an interesting job. She has never had a boyfriend. My friend Ashley has a forgiving and gentle soul. She goes out of her way for everyone she loves and makes the world's best waffles. And yet, as I write this, she is nursing a broken heart. I could go on and on about how fantastic these women are, and how they would make any man very happy. But, at the end of all my examples, I would reveal the same repetitive truth: these beautiful girls – the great catches – don't have boyfriends. They all want boyfriends. They just don't have them. So what's going on? Is anybody out there? A present-day boy whisperer perhaps?

I don't know, maybe it's part of a greater scheme in our

culture nowadays. Maybe people just don't date monogamously as much as they used to in the days of yore. The general consensus in the people I'm surrounded by is that relationships are a rare thing these days, almost an artifact of the past. Maybe this generation will stop getting married, always keeping things too casual for anything serious to ever happen. That would be a total bummer since I've been buying wedding magazines since I was seven years old.

As I've been enchanted by the idea of marriage for so long, and I do believe in love and commitment, I need to trust that there is a light at the end of the tunnel. I need to hold on to hope that this isn't some growing cultural trend, and it isn't that I'm an unlovable loser, either. It's that I'm picking the wrong boys to be the object of my affections. Maybe that's the simple answer, right in front of my nose all along. I don't know, though. I'm not asking to meet Mr. Right. But Mr. Right Now? I've been trying to land him for quite a while. And I guess what I'm trying to figure out is why hasn't it worked out? Why is Mr. Right Now playing so hard to get?

That's the question I'm attempting to tackle, and not just for my sake. I'm doing this on behalf of all the beautiful, wonderful, and unique women in the world who have experienced the emotional roller coaster of "dating," and the frustration of longing for boys who lead them on just to leave them hanging.

In order to do this, I'm going to explore my stories with the men who have made the biggest impression on me – positive or otherwise. The men I liked (or disliked) the most; the men who were the closest of calls or the greatest of mysteries. Some were quick, none were painless, but they were all going seemingly well enough that I *still* wonder what could have been, and why it wasn't. Maybe it's me. Maybe it's them. Maybe it's a combination of both.

Maybe I'll never know.

But even if there's just a slight chance that I may gain some answers – well, then, that's a clarity worth fighting for.

Join me in this pursuit of enlightenment, and together let's try to find some reason in the murky madness.

Hold onto your hats, handkerchiefs, and other various accessories. I think we're in for a bumpy ride.

Here we go.

Justin

My initial introduction of romantic dealings may have been with Ken in kindergarten, but years later, that mere introduction intensified into something more with someone else. There was a boy who didn't just make an introduction – he made an impact.

I'm taking it back to the first boy I really liked. He was the first boy I pictured doing all the delicious relationship things with – hand holding, kissing on the lips, and watching documentaries about Walt Disney. He was the first boy to give me uncontrollable, hyperactive butterflies. He was the first boy who had my soul swooning with complete infatuation. He was the first boy to help me really understand, really *feel* the lyrics to my favorite love songs, inspiring me to belt them out on my Spice Girls karaoke set with a passion previously unknown to me. Dancing around and singing the British girl band's greatest hits was never the same. He spiced up my life.

His name was Justin.

I was a mere sixth grader when Justin first floated into my humble but happy, single, and naïve life. It was the middle of an otherwise mundane academic year when he transferred to my school, and a lot of buzz quickly generated about the new boy. According to gossip on the playground, he was in the eighth grade and a total stud muffin. I was unfazed. The guys who were usually considered "dreamy" amongst the girls at my school were never my type. They were always too obnoxious, too thickheaded, too *average*. So I casually shrugged off the rumors, unaffected by the mysterious new boy's persona. I was an independent, single sixth-grader. Ah, to be that way again. I was so innocent. If only I knew. But I had no idea what was in store for me.

o o o o o

I was sitting at my lunch table in the cafeteria, contentedly eating my heart-shaped whole-wheat peanut butter sandwich, when I first saw him. Yes, *him*. Justin. Oh, Justin. He was, without a doubt, the most exquisite boy I had ever laid eyes on – Disney Channel stars and John Travolta included. Justin was the epitome of sex appeal: tall-for-an-eighth-grader, dark, and handsome. As he stood in the lunch line, with his chocolate brown curls falling tenderly onto his beautiful face, I couldn't stop staring. I got it. I *got* it. I understood the hype, the female hysteria surrounding the new kid. He was simply outstanding.

That first sighting of him in the cafeteria had made up my mind. I was like an explorer, who had just spotted the most magnificent creature in the world – a rare and unique species that she had waited her whole life to discover. Now that I had found him, I couldn't let him just walk away, back into the wilderness. I had a mission, and I would do all that I could to accomplish it. I had to know Justin. And Justin had to know me. It was as simple as that.

Now Justin was an older man: he was in the eighth grade, I was in sixth. It was dangerous and exciting, but it also added a bit of an obstacle in the pathway to his heart. We didn't have classes together or hang out with the same group of friends. He didn't even know I existed. That had to change. That would change! I was a determined little sixth grade sprite.

With creative thinking and a lot of consideration, I developed a plan to get Justin to notice me. Every morning, before the bell rang signaling the start of a new school day, students congregated on the playground. The younger grades played games, chasing each other around and bouncing about. Ah, the carefree naivety of youth. The older, more mature grades would stand in groups and chatter. The eighth graders stood against a big white wall, closest to where they lined up to enter the school building. I noticed Justin standing there every morning, surrounded by his eighth grade male friends, talking about whatever it is that eighth grade homeboys talk about. Women? Rap music? Cars? Existentialism? I don't know. I didn't care, either, Justin just looked so goddamn beautiful doing it. And so, considering this co-mingling of the grades every morning, my plan was hatched.

In order to perfectly execute my stratagem, I woke up every morning at 6:00 a.m. to freshly shower, wash and blow dry my hair, primp, and make myself look as beautiful, stylish, and funky fresh as possible. As a sixth grader, I didn't wear makeup, but I did wear the heck out of some strawberry flavored chap stick. Classic. Then, I was dropped off a little earlier to the playground, as Justin always arrived on the early side as well. Once there, I found my way to my BFF who knew of my super-crush on Justin: Teddy. She and I would then walk, all along the giant track circle that was painted onto the pavement, and talk. We moved past the younger children frolicking, and of course, past the white wall crowded with eighth graders... one handsome, male eighth grader in particular.

The first couple of mornings, I was too shy to look over at him as we passed, which gained me criticism from Teddy. But she didn't understand. The point of our cardio observation was not to smile at him, or do anything else flashy like that. It was to get him to notice my presence, and maybe fall in love with me at first sight. However, I could see Teddy's point, and reasoned that it wouldn't hurt to, at the very least, glance in his general direction the next morning.

No, it did not hurt at all. The next day, though nervous,

I casually glanced towards the big white wall as Teddy and I approached. I felt my cheeks immediately flush a hot pink color as I saw a pair of deep, dark brown eyes staring back at me: Justin's eyes. My heart danced as our eyes locked, that moment of contact solidifying my soul's desirous suspicions. I didn't hear a word of what Teddy was babbling about beside me, because it was then that I realized it was my middle-school destiny to be with Justin. We were romantic perfection just waiting to happen.

o o o o o

Later that day, we had a school assembly of some sort. To be honest, I can't remember the occasion, probably because I was too enveloped in a more specific detail of the event, namely, Justin's presence. During the nondescript assembly, he sang for the whole student body, and hypnotized me with his angelic voice. When he finished his melodious tune, I sprang to my feet with the rest of the auditorium, vigorously clapping my hands in praise. I had never seen or heard anything so perfect before. Looks AND talent? What a dime.

Quite conveniently, after the discovery of Justin's amazing set of pipes, my mom told me that she was organizing an after-school group of students, intended to offer help, inspiration, and guidance in honing their passions. She wanted to gather students from a variety of grades, and told my sister, who was in third grade at the time, and me, to pick a couple of our friends to participate. My mom also had a friend whose son was in the eighth grade and would be joining the group, along with a friend of his. My ears perked up at this fortuitous news. Eighth graders, eh? I had the perfect eighth grade candidate for this group: a boy with a wonderful gift and a promising future, and looks to boot. Not that my mom cared about the last part, but she knew how much I liked him and that he was truly talented, so she gave his mother a call.

I was overjoyed when my mother later shared the news with me that Justin would be joining our group. And not only was he joining the group, but he also had to come home with us on Wednesdays and stay until 7:00 p.m., when his mother got off work and could come pick him up. My jaw dropped as my mom revealed that last bit of information. I could not have gotten better news. This meant that Justin and I would be eating dinner together, one night a week. Romance over a candlelit dinner shared with the object of my affection and also my mom and sister? Yes, please!

My trajectory for Justin and me falling in love over weekly dinners and after-school activities didn't pan out quite as quickly as I would've liked. I soon found out that Justin was the strong, silent type. Very silent. During the first couple of meetings, we didn't say anything to each other, not even "hi" or "hello." On the drive back to my house, it was my mom he exchanged pleasantries with, not me. I was more than a little discouraged. How were we supposed to fall in love if we never spoke?

My mom tried to encourage me, saying that sometimes it took time to get to know a person — but hey, on the bright side, Liam seemed to take a liking to me! It was true, not that it soothed my aching heart. Liam was my mom's friend's son, and he did smile at me a lot. He even winked at me a couple of times and once gave me a Godiva chocolate bar. While I very much appreciated the attention, and especially the chocolate, I still yearned for things to work out with Justin. I could not be swayed by Liam's wily charms, much to my mother's dismay. To this day, she pines after Liam on my behalf as the one that got away, despite his player status and plethora of angel tattoos.

o o o o o

About a month into the program, it finally happened: the moment of connection with the true object of my affection, sweet and shy Justin. I remember feeling especially brave one day and asking him about one of our school's famous eighth grade English projects. Students were required to create posters for the movies of their lives, and once complete, they were hung up around the hallways. As soon as they were displayed, I spared no time finding Justin's project, and it did not disappoint. It was creative and witty, including rave reviews "authored" by celebrity chefs, which of course was supposed to be ironic because he wasn't a chef and the movie had nothing to do with food. Okay, so maybe it wasn't entirely brilliant, but at the time, I'd never seen anything finer. Plus, it featured a nicely sized picture of his face, so that alone made it flawless to me. After dinner one Wednesday night, I complimented him on it. He seemed really appreciative, and was responsive when I asked him some questions about it. That led to him asking me questions about my classes, and just like that, the ice was broken, and I started swimming through the piercingly cold waters towards the warmth of Justin's heart.

o o o o o

As the weeks progressed, Justin and I developed a really great rapport and a solid friendship. The silence between us was effectively shattered; in fact, all we did was talk. It was so easy to talk to him about anything and everything: school, movies, books, music. He made me laugh, and was really nice to my pet rabbit, Edward. What more could a girl ask for? Every Wednesday night, we shared warm Italian dinners, and I marveled as he proved to me that he could fit an entire ravioli in his mouth, without cutting it. What a hunk of man. I was smitten.

Our involvement in my mom's group only strengthened my feelings for Justin. For one of the group meetings, I baked cookies with mini M&M's in them. When Justin bit into one, he exclaimed, "Sweet!" in approval. I swear I thought my heart would burst. We did several community service events at senior living centers, where we visited with residents and put on a show for them. In addition to having her own law practice, my mom also owned a dance academy, and my sister and I took classes there, so we performed a dance or two from our favorite classes with a couple of other girls who were also both in the group and in dance with us. And, of course, Justin would sing. He always sang a solo, to the same song: "This I Promise You" by *NSYNC.

It was so beautiful, so romantic, so swoon-worthy. His heavenly voice ringing out with lyrics of such love and devotion positively hypnotized me. During the four-minute performance, I would tune out everyone else in the room, pretending he was singing only to me.

o o o o o

As time went on, crawling closer and closer to Justin's eighth grade graduation, I grew more and more anxious. Justin wasn't going to school nearby: he was going to a highly esteemed high school in New York City. He was going to commute every day, which eased my concern a little because I figured if we started dating, we could see each other on the weekends. I could only assume that was the direction our relationship was headed in – we were great friends and confidents to one another, we made each other laugh, and shared excellent conversation. I figured it was only a matter of time before Justin admitted that he had deeply overwhelming feelings for me, and we'd embark upon one of the greatest love affairs of all time.

Yet, to my great disappointment, there was no grand declaration of love made on his behalf. There came no official request to keep in touch, no asking me to accompany him to the movies or to the beach or the soda shop sometime over the summer. I didn't even get a hug filled with tenderness and the promise of things to come. I was upset and confused: I really got the vibe that we liked each other. But his graduation came and went, and left me in the dust. I didn't see Justin all summer, and it didn't get any better in the fall. This was before the time of Facebook, even before texting really took off as a valid form of communication. With only instant messaging and snail mail to keep us intact, we sort of just... grew apart. He became really involved and busy with high school, and didn't reach out. I was also really involved and busy, being the president of my self-started "Harry Potter" fan club, and couldn't reach out as often as I would have liked. I sent him a couple of friendly but casual instant messages, which he answered, but the conversations that ensued were short and simple. I gave up after a while, as I didn't want to be a pest.

Justin kind of just faded out of my life. I was sad. Really sad. I thought we'd keep in touch, fall in love, and be high school sweethearts. We'd follow in the footsteps of my grandparents, who fell in love in high school, and stayed in love, eventually getting married and having babies and vacationing in Hawaii. He and I would slow dance to *NSYNC, he could serenade our children to sleep, and we'd grow old together, always sharing ravioli dinners on Wednesday nights.

But that didn't happen. I never saw Justin again. He made a brief re-appearance in my life, freshman year of high school, when I finally rejoined the rest of the world and got a Facebook profile. Curiosity got the best of me and I searched for him, I admit it. I found him, as handsome as ever, and after doing a light scan of his pictures and relationship status, saw that he was single. Feeling particularly brazen and confident in my newly appointed profile picture of me attempting to model in my grandparents' basement, I did it: I friend requested him. My heart leapt up into my throat when he accepted my virtual friendship. Perhaps this was our second chance at eternal love. I sent him a "hey, how's life been?" message, which he quickly replied to, and we shared a brief but scintillating catch-up conversation. I may have gotten slightly carried away with my expectations, once again. My first year at an all-girls' high school wasn't proving to be especially fruitful in the boy department, so I fell back into an old habit. The Justin habit, specifically. But it was soon clear that our relationship was going no further than our initial catch-up session and I had to resign myself to that fact. It wasn't easy, as I had to let go of Justin a second time.

o o o o o

Last time I checked, according to my Facebook newsfeed, Justin graduated from college and moved to Los Angeles to pursue a singing career. I caved and watched a couple of the videos he posted as a part of his online resume. He is still really handsome, and really talented. Damn him. We could have shared something beautiful. Not to mention, I love Los Angeles and have been keeping my eyes open for the perfect dress to wear to the Grammys for forever, you know, in case he were to be super successful. It would be daring and sexy à la J.Lo's plunging Puff Daddy-era neckline, with the fashion and elegance of a gown that Grace Kelly would wear. I would make it on the best-dressed list, for sure. Also, if he won a Grammy and inevitably thanked his angel goddess of a girlfriend – me – for being his one true muse and inspiration, and the reason he even breathes, I have the perfect humble/full of love/also very proud facial expression on point so that when the camera panned to me in the audience, everyone watching in America would sigh collectively at our magical love. But I guess it just wasn't in the stars. I don't know why not – but it's fine. I wish him the best. May he sell a million copies of a platinum album or at least be a one hit wonder. Whatever.

Is Justin the one that got away? Well, he's certainly not the one who stayed, and I still don't really understand why. We both had genuinely wonderful conversation and shared a love of Italian food. That's not exactly easy to find these days, especially with everyone going vegan and gluten-free. But hey, que sera sera. I loved the time I spent with Justin, and will always think on it fondly, though I don't think our paths are destined to intertwine again. Justin was the first of many to get my hopes up in love, and then, just when I thought something big was going to happen, he disappeared, and it ended. Even though I've been practicing this song and dance since the sixth grade, I still haven't gotten quite used to it just yet.

Adam

I'VE ALWAYS FOUND IT INTIMIDATING, TALKING to cute boys. In general, I'm a pretty friendly and outgoing person, but when put in front of a beautiful boy whom I think it would be nice to kiss, my instinct is to clam up like a girl who was just told that if she ever spoke again, *The Walking Dead* would be canceled and Rick and Daryl would be violently killed in the series finale.

What if I say something stupid? What if my laugh comes out too enthusiastically and I snort like an unattractive buffoon? What if I let something slip that I only know about him because I intensively stalked his social media accounts? These are just some of the concerns that flicker through my mind whilst verbally engaging with an attractive male human.

It tends to get easier the more you get to know the guy, as he progresses from "stranger I'm attracted to" to "acquaintance I have cool exchanges with" to "we're buddies I think" to "friends – definitely friends" to "don't want to over exaggerate but we're super close/probably best friends" to, well I assume the next step is "radical he's my boyfriend," but clearly I've never gotten that far into the system.

The summer before I went to high school, I entered into

the "stranger I'm attracted to" phase with the stud who moved into the house behind mine. A few weeks past the move-in, he mowed his backyard – shirtless. I first noticed him while I was walking to the kitchen to score a muffin for breakfast. Instantly intrigued by the half-naked hunk in such close proximity to me, I dropped the muffin and headed to my backyard to water a garden that didn't exist so I could get a better look at his physique.

I watched him as he moved in perfect horizontal lines back and forth across his overgrown green lawn. A sexy look of determination graced his classically attractive face. He had spikey black hair with frosted tips; it made him look like a handsome mini-wheat. Drop by tantalizing drop, sweat trickled down his face and onto his exposed pecks. I suspect even if it weren't nearly ninety degrees outside, I would have been producing enough nervous sweat to fill a tiny reservoir.

Just as my imaginary garden had been about ten minutes overwatered, a voice from inside the new neighbors' house yelled: "Adam!" The sexy landscaping teen – apparently named Adam – turned, and shut off his lawnmower before disappearing into his garage.

o o o o o

I started spending a lot of time in my backyard over the following couple of weeks. Adam was almost always in his backyard, either mowing the lawn sans shirt or riding his dirt bike in circles around the house. One time, after finishing his eighth lap around the house's perimeter on his dirt bike, Adam took off his helmet and happened to catch my gaze from where I was kneeling, "pretending" to "plant" some "tomatoes." (To be honest I just grabbed some uncooked rice from our cabinets and buried it beneath the dirt.) My entire body shivered (even though it was brutally hot out) when he flashed me a crooked grin with his shockingly white teeth. I really think they may have sparkled. Sure, it could've just been the sun's rays reflecting off his teeth's surfaces, but I believe it was the magic of Adam's charm, coupled with his impeccable oral hygiene. He followed the grin with a wink and I was actually thankful for all of the space in between us, because my face turned the color of an actual tomato, not my fake rice vegetable.

After waiting the appropriate amount of time – so as to not look like a crazed and smitten lunatic – I ran into my house and lightly suggested an idea to my mother. And by "lightly suggested an idea," I mean that I forced my mother to host a fabulous summer barbecue at our house and invite the new neighbors so that Adam and I could spend quality time together and eventually fall in love.

My mother has always been an angel in trying to aid my love life, akin to Cupid, so a couple of weeks later I found myself waking up on the day of the casual summer barbecue that was going to cook up more than meats and potato salad, if you catch my drift. My drift is that it was going to cook up chemistry between Adam and me. I couldn't have been more excited. I spent the morning at the hair salon, where my locks were styled identically to Hilary Duff's in a picture I cut out of one of those peace-love-girl-stuff magazines. I needed to look like a total hotcake for my time with Adam.

The night came, and I was ready. My heart sang when I saw Adam walk through our front door. His frosted tips looked especially coiffed, and I couldn't help but wonder if we both spent extra time on our hair that day in an effort to impress each other. Before I could greet him hello, my bestie from next-door, Kimberly, arrived, and I watched Adam walk to my backyard as she and my sister talked about how delicious the lemonade looked.

A few minutes later, I couldn't find Adam. He wasn't in the backyard, and he wasn't inside the house. Confused, and concerned that he went home early, I walked towards the front of my house. As I rounded the corner near my front steps, I saw him. Adam was sitting by himself on one of the steps, fiddling with his phone. This was my chance. I could feel my heart beat faster and faster as I approached him. My mind raced trying to come up with cool conversation topics and settle on a good opening line. "Hi, Adam." That's what I decided on. I nodded to myself in affirmation as I was about twenty steps away from him.

I had fifteen steps to go. *I can do this. I can do this*, I thought.

Ten steps to go. *Hi Adam! Hi, Adam. Hi. Adam.*

Five steps to go. *It's going to be okay. What's the worst that could happen? No, seriously, what's the worst that could happen?!*

One step to go. *No. No. No. Keep walking. DON'T STOP!*

And I walked straight past Adam, taking about one hundred more steps to my backyard.

I walked around my entire house two more times, circling past Adam twice. Each time I was too scared to stop, too nervous to talk to him. After the third time passing him, I just decided to stay in the backyard, drinking lemonade with my sister and Kimberly, like a cowardly crawfish. At the end of the night, as we were cleaning up watermelon carcasses and pie plates, my mother was very disheartened and mildly frustrated that I didn't speak to Adam at all at the barbecue fabricated for the sole purpose of our communicating.

Communication between Adam and I never started up. A few months later, his family abruptly moved. Adam, who would seductively mow the backyard whilst shirtless, was replaced by Stanford, a wrinkly 75 year old man who liked to sunbathe in a speedo in the backyard.

Sometimes I wonder what might've been if I had the courage to speak to Adam that fateful night of the neighborly barbecue. Would he have transitioned from "stranger I'm attracted to" into "we're buddies I think" and then eventually "radical he is my boyfriend"? Perhaps. Perhaps it is my own cowardice that has kept me officially single for so long. Perhaps if back then I had the gumption to say, "Hi, Adam," he would be my boyfriend right now. Instead of hanging out with my dog and watching videos on YouTube of Juan Pablo as the Bachelor, I'd be climbing some mountain in the arctic with Adam, shivering on the outside but perfectly warm on the inside because I had a cute and sexy boyfriend who owned a badass dirt bike and bought me sensible boots for arctic mountain climbing. But as my dog drools on my lap and I watch a blonde woman cry because she didn't get a rose from Juan Pablo, I realize how far I am from that scenario.

It's probably for the best. Dirt bikes are like super danger-ous, right? I'm safer this way. Single, but safer.

Mike

IF JUSTIN WAS MY FIRST REAL CRUSH, then Mike was my first real experience with love and lust... an affair to remember, if you will. A non-labeled affair, that is. To quote my friend Charles Dickens[1], it was the best of times, and it was the worst of times: a roller coaster of emotions. But I enjoyed every minute of the ride, ultimately. Key word here being *ultimately*. At the time of our fine affair, I couldn't wrap my head around why we would never seal the deal – and make our relationship official. Where was his "be my girlfriend and therefore my forever queen" proposal posed in skywriting, followed by an unbreakable promise that he'd love me eternally? Hindsight is 20/20, but back in the day, I was left confused and heartbroken.

I remember the first time I ever laid eyes on Mike, clear as the day is blue (or whatever the best expression is for remembering every exact detail of a particular event in your life). I had just turned seventeen, and was in need of a dance partner for the upcoming competition season. Side note: my partner at the time was Morgan, a scrawny 16 year old whose mom forced him to take up breakdance. The world of dance competition was

---

1   We've never met... or spoken... or been alive at the same time. We aren't friends.

fierce, and having a partner who was shorter than me with – to quote our choreographer – "noodle arms" was a surefire way to be a LOSER, so poor Morgan had to be replaced. I had always dreamed of having a really strong, sexy, masculine dance partner, à la Channing Tatum in *Step Up*... someone to share chemistry with both on and off the dance floor, if you know what I'm saying. However, for whatever unjust reason, there seemed to be a shortage of rugged dancing men in my area. Or so I thought. I would soon come to know that my solution managed the local pizzeria, not five minutes from the location of the dance studio.

My family lived and worked in a fairly small town, and my mom's law office was just a few blocks away from said pizzeria. The pizza there was the best in town, and so my mom would often walk there for lunch. After going several times, she became friendly with the manager, Mike, who was known for two things: dazzling customer service and the most amazing, cheesy pizza. He was a pepperoni pro. In getting to know Mike, who was quite social and quite the conversationalist, my mom eventually shared with him that she ran a dance academy, and, in turn, Mike revealed that he was a dancer – a hip hop dancer, that is – and had performed in several music videos and fashion shows. I can only imagine that a few break dance fights were sprinkled in amongst his list of performances as well, or maybe now I'm just really trying to mold him into the Channing Tatum/*Step Up* image. Mike loved the art of dance: it was his passion. Pizza was just his day job. My mother could not wait to share the news with me. She had found him! My new dance partner! The next best thing to Channing Tatum!

I was thrilled when I heard the news, and almost thought it was too good to be true. I had never seen Mike myself, but my mom assured me that he was good-looking in a rugged, edgy way. That was enough to get me on board. I've always had a thing for bad boys, ever since I fell in love with Danny Zuko as portrayed by John Travolta in *Grease*. So we made plans with my choreographer, Jenna, to recruit Mike the following week, hoping that he'd sign right up and slide onto the dance floor with me.

I remember everything about that fateful day so perfectly. My body was rattled with nervous energy as we stood, waiting for the light to turn green so we could cross the street and start the journey towards the pizzeria. Walking in the damp weather, my mom and Jenna laughed as they reminisced about how we all first met. I chuckled along distractedly, my nerves meandering my attention instead to the soggy leaves squishing underneath my feet. I was worried the weather might ruin my appearance before Mike saw me, and I only wanted the best first impression between my new potential dance partner and me. I dressed to impress, wearing my favorite, new, dark blue dress, a white leather watch encrusted with hundreds of faux diamonds, and a sexy black lace bra that was super uncomfortable but made me feel confident.

We finally approached the pizza place. I walked in and locked eyes for the first time with Mike.

As soon as the little bell on the door rang, signaling our entrance, he looked up, and right at me. My heart did a little flip as our gazes locked, and I noticed he seemed particularly interested in my sudden appearance in his land of pizza. I was so happy. He was perfect. My very own Channing Tatum. Taller than me, and sexy indeed, with swagger oozing out of his every pore. Noodle arms? More like caboodle arms! I'm not sure what this means. His were strong and shapely – the furthest thing from spaghetti. He had short brown hair, full lips, an athletic build, and grey eyes. He was definitely rough-around-the-edges, and appeared super confident as he greeted my mom, his gaze still darting back to me every so often. My mom introduced Jenna, and then went into the whole spiel. When she gestured to me, her daughter who was in need of a dance partner, he looked me up and down subtly. After sharing a couple more details with him, Mike quickly agreed to shake his groove thing with me. Before I knew it, I was pulling out my hot pink Razor flip phone to add him to my contacts and give him my number in return. For scheduling purposes, of course. When he heard my name, he said:

"Lorraine, huh? See you Monday, Lorraine."

He walked to the back donning a sexy smile and I floated out of there on a cloud. I had never before so eagerly anticipated a Monday.

○ ○ ○ ○ ○

Monday's initial rehearsal came and went pretty smoothly, but, then again, not too smoothly at all. It was smooth in the sense that Mike and I connected instantly, and I knew it wouldn't be hard for me to emote chemistry with him on the dance floor, as there was already so much chemistry between us in real life. So, flirtation-wise, it was a very smooth rehearsal. Technique-wise, it was a little bit of a bumpy start. It turns out, Mike may have exaggerated his dancing abilities, much to the frustration of Jenna. He was resistant to actually dance in front of me, and seemed a little nervous. He didn't move much at all. Jenna gave most of the work to me, which I didn't mind one bit. I wanted a chance to show off my talents to Mike, so sue me. Jenna wasn't happy with this arrangement, though. By the end of the rehearsal, she demanded that Mike dance some sort of solo for her, to prove he could actually handle the task at hand. Feeling a little embarrassed on his behalf, I excused myself from the room, and, to this day, I have no idea what Mike showed Jenna in that time. Though I did decide that rehearsals might be better if they happened privately between Mike and me, with Jenna and I meeting separately so I could learn the routine, and then pass the choreography on to Mike at our rehearsals. No hidden agenda whatsoever! Or so a better, stronger version of myself would insist. I didn't want to let go of Mike as a partner, no matter what happened when he showed Jenna his moves. I was already in too deep. I didn't care if he could only do the chicken dance. I would make it work. If they could do it in the movies, we could do it in real life.

○ ○ ○ ○ ○

Mondays quickly became my favorite day of the week. Mike and I continued to meet for "rehearsals," and I use quotation marks around rehearsals because we honestly didn't do much rehearsing. The chemistry between us only grew, and kept getting hotter and hotter as each week progressed. The hour started innocently enough, with me attempting to show him the first step in the dance. It was just unfortunate that this step required him and I to stand face-to-face, with our hands touching. The scenario set us up perfectly for our favorite past time: staring dreamily into each other's eyes. He thought I had the most beautiful blue eyes in the world, and complimented me on them vehemently.

"Are you sure you don't wear contacts? Those can't be your real eyes!" he'd say in wonderment.

It felt like he was staring straight through my eyes and into my soul. It was dizzying. If he wasn't marveling at my eyes, he was finding some other way to make me feel like the most beautiful woman in the world, telling me I was gorgeous and sexy, and that he'd never met anyone like me before.

And I had definitely never met anyone like *him* before. In addition to flirting outrageously, we also talked a lot in rehearsals – about everything – and we had a lot of similar interests, surprisingly. I say surprisingly because the more I learned about Mike the more I realized how different we were, and how we came from two entirely different places. To me, he was the manifestation of a bad boy from the wrong side of the tracks. He grew up in a very dangerous neighborhood. I think he graduated high school, but that was never made perfectly clear to me. He was street-smart, ghetto, gangster, a badass. He was always telling me about another brother or sister who he was constantly getting out of trouble, bailing out of jail, defending in street fights, etc. He had the battle wounds to prove it, and in one rehearsal, he showed me all the places he had scars from being either shot or stabbed. He credited his boss at the pizzeria with cleaning him up. What that means he never really did say; I tend to think he had some sort of indiscretions in his past relating to drugs or prison or both. He had roughly half a dozen tattoos. At the time, I thought they were incredibly sexy. He had Chinese writing on one forearm, which translated to read: "POWER." On his other forearm was a "R.I.P. Tupac" tattoo. A tiger graced one of his biceps, and his biggest tattoo rested in huge cursive letters on his back, spelling out with love his daughter's name. Yes, Mike had a daughter, something else I quickly learned about him. He didn't talk much about the mother, and I didn't ask much about the mother. But I knew he had a cute little girl and two pit bulls that he loved more than life itself. He didn't have a car and walked everywhere he went, and smoked like one of those factories that pollute so much thick, black smoke in the air it's causing global warming. As you may have already assumed, he was a tad older than me at twenty-one years old, but I didn't mind. I didn't mind any of it. I was so wrapped up in Mike that I was able to look past all of these... red flags, if you will. Plus, he was so much more than a couple of red flags. He was caring and funny. He took a genuine interest in my life and my family. I taught a class of young girls at the studio, right after my rehearsals with Mike, and he was so nice to all of my students. He charmed them like he charmed me, making them laugh and feel special. He complimented them on their dancing and me on my choreography. Beyond that, he and I both loved ensemble comedy films centered on the Christmas holidays and shared a common interest in Shakespeare's work. Mike was a complicated man: one who both appreciated *Hamlet* and got into violent knife fights on the streets.

o o o o o

After a short while, I started to move our relationship out of the studio and into the pizza place. It was a great way for me to have more time with him, and see him at work in his element. Mike was fantastic at his job, and the best employee in the whole pizzeria. He loved to show off his skills, especially when I was there, and would flip and juggle knives and dough and sauce like a brilliant showman as he prepared pizzas, his eyes rarely leaving mine. I was mesmerized. It was a riveting and sexy display of pizza making. I also began hosting little holiday parties for my dance class students at the pizzeria. There was a small area to the side of the restaurant with tables, and I'd come in early to set up for the party, and Mike would always help me with anything I needed – especially with the trickiest part a.k.a. the tablecloth. He was very attentive and helpful, like a doting, masculine party-planning assistant whose bones I wanted to jump. I made my own desserts to bring for the girls to enjoy after their pizza, with the hope that Mike would try one of the confections and like me even more. Yet, every time I offered him one, he declined, saying he didn't like sweets, which frustrated me to no end. I truly thought him eating one of my brownies would bewitch him into kissing me. But otherwise, Mike and I shined at those parties. We were a great team, entertaining the girls and keeping the party nice and lively. The girls always had a fantastic time, and so did I. Mike did too, I think.

However, as much as the pizzeria was a backdrop of joy for our budding relationship, it was also the site of drama, one distinctive, horrible time. I was in the pizzeria with my sister and cousins; we were grabbing a quick bite to eat before heading off to see the classic Vince Vaughn Christmas film, *Fred Claus*. As we were paying, Mike was teasing me for collecting Mariah Carey t-shirts, saying he was too old to collect things. Now, mind you, at the time he had no idea how old I was. I replied that you could never be too old to collect things, and I suppose it was there that Mike saw his chance to scout information.

"Well, how old are you?" Mike asked.

My heart stopped. I panicked and I realized I couldn't take too long to answer, but also realized that the truth might have cost me a future with Mike.

"Nineteen," I answered as coolly as I could.

Mike seemed happy with my answer, but the second I was out the door and air started to fill my lungs again, my cousin – the moral compass of the evening – asked me why I didn't tell Mike my real age. I felt horribly guilty, but I didn't want Mike losing interest in me because I was younger than him. I liked him too much to risk losing him. But my lie nagged at me throughout the entire movie, and I couldn't be distracted no matter how sexy Vince Vaughn looked in a Santa suit. I had never pulled off anything so deceptive or rebellious in my life. This was unchartered territory.

o o o o o

A couple of weeks later, the moment I had been anticipating for months finally arrived. Mike and I were rehearsing, a very *Step Up*-esque move where I was standing on one leg, and he was holding my other leg under my knee. I was about to show him how I was going to get out of that position, which required him letting my leg down. In an effort to be playful, he refused to let go, and I was pretending to be frustrated. When I asked him why he wouldn't let me go, he replied, every so suavely:

"I don't want to."

And then, before I knew it, he was going in for the kiss. In retrospect, it was kind of corny; at the time, it made me weak in the knees.

Our first kiss was a bit of a surreal moment for me. It was something I had been anticipating for so long, something I had been building up so much in my mind over time. Our first kiss was also my first kiss ever, and that alone was a little overwhelming. Especially when you consider the circumstances, the circumstances being it was awful. Really sloppy. Really long. Really too much. It just kept going and going and going. I tried pulling away a few times, hoping to come up for air, but he must've just interpreted that as part of my technique, because nothing stopped him. Little did he know, I had no technique, and was desperate for some sort of lifesaver or arm floaties to help me from drowning in his mouth. It was way too much to handle for a first kiss. Eventually, after what seemed like hours, he pulled away, rested his forehead against mine, and chuckled ever so slightly before smiling. I smiled, too, because after all, it was what I wanted for the longest time, and it finally happened. It was like the ending of a Jason Derulo music video. Except oddly I wasn't delighted by it. I forget what was said immediately afterwards, but I do remember feeling flustered or distracted later on, and then giggling and covering my face in my hands, playing it off as being distracted by our "dreamy" kiss. He chuckled cockily. If only he knew what was really racing through my mind at the time. As we ended rehearsal, more people came into the studio, thankfully erasing any chances of us sharing another make out session.

I had just kissed the guy I was crazy about, shouldn't I have been ecstatic? On top of the world? Throwing rose petals at random strangers whilst singing sweet words of love and promises? But I wasn't. All I could think about was how weird it was, and overwhelming. I tossed and turned all night, dissecting the kiss. What did it mean? Did I not like Mike anymore? Was it awkward because it was my first kiss, and caught me unaware? Was Mike just a bad kisser? I was also upset because he had taken my first kiss and slobbered all over it. For years, I had been dreaming about my first kiss: what it would be like, how it would feel. In all of my fantasies, it was never as it turned out to be with Mike. In my fantasies, it was the perfect kiss: romantic, passionate, and dreamy. I ended the kiss with stars in my eyes and a patter in my heart, exhilarated and craving more. It was sweet and straight out of a buttery rom-com, laced with promise and desire. Essentially, it was almost the polar opposite of my actual first kiss with Mike. I cringed thinking of the awkward and wet tale I'd be sharing with my children, my friends, strangers on the street who might stop and ask me what my first kiss was like. I would have to reveal to them the slobbery truth, how I missed out on a perfect experience of such a classic milestone. (In retrospect, I am very pleased by my Jason Derulo-esque first kiss experience, no matter how much Mike's tongue was overused in the duration of it.)

Just as the sun started to rise, I managed to calm myself down. Everything would be fine! I just had to take it step by step with Mike. The bad kiss didn't mean anything. There was definitely room for improvement. Adjusted and resolute in this way of thinking, I geared myself up for my next rehearsal with Mike, determined to enjoy our next kiss.

Little did I know just how unnecessary my stoic determination to go forth with Mike was; he showed up to the rehearsal following our kiss limping and complaining of a leg injury. While jumping in front of a car to save his dog from meeting an untimely end, he pulled or tore something in his leg, and would be unable to dance. He was sorry. He felt bad. But there was no way he'd be able to finish the dance, let alone compete or perform it a bunch of times after that. His brother picked him up a few minutes later in a purple car, and as Mike left I told his brother to take good care of him. His brother looked rather confused and asked for clarification before Mike quickly told him to forget about it. Was I suspicious of this so-called injury? Hells yes. But I was also relieved because I really didn't know how he and I were going to pull off an entire competition-worthy routine, considering he was lying from the start about his hip-hop video dance skills. So Danny stepped in and saved the day. Danny taught at the studio, and he is the best Michael Jackson impersonator I've ever seen. We knocked out an amazing routine together to the King of Pop's "P.Y.T." and the crowd went wild. It was critically acclaimed by my grandparents and other members of the studio community, and was the favorite routine of the season for many. And while I'd like to tell you that Danny and I fell in love and got married – as certain people did ask me whether we were together because of our steamy onstage chemistry – we are both quite single. He's like the goofy older brother I never had, and so we remain ever in a deep friendship-love of a lifetime.

Surprisingly, the leg incident was not the end of the road for Mike and me. We saw each other rather frequently, as I continued to have an appetite for pizza and he remained a presence in the studio, in a more behind-the-scenes way. My heart was warmed and my flu weakened when he made me chicken soup after my mom went into the pizza place and told him I was feeling under the weather. During "Observation Week" at the studio, I invited him to sit in on the class that I taught, and he came looking really gorgeous in a deep red long sleeve top. He also wore diamond studs in his ears. They were flashy but oddly enticing.

When the class was over, we walked a little bit outside, and shared a brief kiss before he disappeared into the night. Like Batman. He helped me out another time with a project at the studio: I was choreographing a male/female dance for tweens, and the boys were especially rambunctious and hard to control. Mike happily came to rehearsals to keep the boys in line. My feelings for him remained, though I was frustrated because he never asked me out on a date. We saw each other all the time, but it was always in some sort of a professional circumstance. Though between school and the dance academy, I was too busy to dwell on it, and so we continued on into the summer season at the same consistent, low key/not a relationship pace.

I lost my patience about a month into the summer. I was done waiting. It didn't make any sense; it was obvious that he liked me. On a day where I felt particularly brazen, I went to the pizzeria during its slow time, and asked Mike if he'd like to see a movie with me. He said sure. I was so happy and relieved. I'm not sure I was ready to handle face-to-face rejection. Later, over text, we arranged to see the latest Will Smith movie. Then, thirty minutes before we were supposed to meet, he cancelled with some bogus excuse. He needed to help get one of his sisters somewhere for something... I don't know. It was far-fetched, kind of like the time he dove in front of a moving vehicle for his dog, sustained a serious injury, and then miraculously – under forty-eight hours later – his limp disappeared. I was outraged and so disappointed. I had picked out the perfect first date outfit, and even selected the perfect first date movie snack, in the event he decided to get popcorn: Junior Mints, as they would be both satisfying and breath freshening. My sweet tooth would've been contented and my breath crisp and minty, ready for true love's kiss. Well so much for that.

The next morning, I was happily surprised when Mike texted me to reschedule our date. It was hard to get truly excited about it, though. The whole day, I waited with bated breath, anticipating the worst. Every time my phone buzzed, I assumed it was his cancellation text, signaling his deep loathing of me. I so did not want to get that text. But, much to my relief, that text never came, and I found myself walking to the movie theatre at our pre-scheduled time. As I approached the front doors, I saw him standing there, and my heart stopped. I was already excited to be finally going on an official date with Mike, and I had a feeling our date would exceed my expectations from the moment I saw him there.

It was an amazing date, one of the best dates I've ever been on, to this day. He looked so handsome, dressed in a white button-up shirt and dark jeans. When he leaned in to give me a kiss on the cheek in greeting, he smelled amazing – so manly and delicious. As the night proceeded, he was so chivalrous, opening doors for me and paying for everything. We sat in the back of the dark theatre and barely watched the movie. He spent the entire time leaning in towards me, whispering in my ear. He told me he had never met anyone like me, and that no one ever treated him as nicely as I did. When the movie was over, we walked around town a bit, and somehow ended up in front of the dance academy. We stood there, talking for quite a while, until he had to go home to feed his pit bulls. He leaned in and kissed me, and it was the most perfect, wonderful kiss in the whole world. I mean, the total opposite of our first make out session. As we stood there kissing, I hoped we would never stop. At one point, Mike reluctantly pulled away and smirked before saying:

"I better go, before you get me all excited."

I hoped my outside face didn't portray what my insides were feeling, which was: cool! I made a boy excited with my lips! I tried to maintain a confident and apparently-good-kisser attitude as I stood on my tiptoes and gave Mike one last final kiss. He smiled down at me and said goodnight. And so was the perfect end to a perfect date.

I floated home on a cloud that evening, the date playing on a constant loop in my head to the sounds of romantic music sung by Taylor Swift or Boyz II Men. I was in a heavenly state of euphoria. That night, I was out – in public – with a boy: a sexy male friend whose lips I touched with my lips. Mike and I were like a couple, being seen by the world like a couple. Canoodling in the back of the movie theatre? Check. Making out in public? Check. My head sunk into my pillow and I sighed to myself as I thought that evening, there was probably some little girl walking around town who spotted Mike and me. She probably watched us dreamily, admiring how our individual, unique-but-both-sexy styles blended together to create such an enviably good-looking couple. She probably started to daydream about the day she'd meet her own Mike, and go out on a date with him and make some other little girl envious in the same way she was right then. I was a relationship inspiration to some lovely, cherubic girl that evening. I was her hero, her role model, someone she'd remember forever or at least until she next went to the toy store or the Gymboree. And even if there wasn't a little girl there was at least one person, one human – or hell – one bird flying about who saw Mike and I together that night as a couple. That person or bird might've even assumed we were boyfriend and girlfriend. To me, it was downright thrilling. I felt sexy, like a daring vixen of a goddess who had a badass hunk of a man by her side. Man, I felt like a woman! It's how I imagine those Victoria's Secret models feel when they're bouncing around in the underwear commercials.

Following our date, Mike and I texted and talked on the phone often. It was always flirtatious, and always exciting, but he had yet to ask me out on another date, which of course, confused me. After a couple of weeks, I threw caution to the wind, and asked him again. He said yes, and I bought a new purse for the occasion. Purple leopard print patterned, of course: perfect second date material. However, I stood alone that night in front of the movie theatre, practically pacing as I waited for him to show. Fifteen minutes past the time he was supposed to be there, he called to tell me he had lost his wallet. He wouldn't be able to pay. He couldn't make it. I said that I would get our tickets this time, and told him to come anyway. He resisted, insisting that he was the man and he should pay. After a little bit more convincing on my part, he finally agreed to come. But he never showed up.

Mike never called or texted me to explain. When I went into the pizzeria a few days later, he acted as though nothing had ever happened. I was devastated. And so ended our little affair, without rhyme or reason.

o o o o o

A couple of months later, I was in the pizza place with my sister and cousins, and so was he. Once my homies were seated and waiting for their pizza, Mike and I were alone. I pretended I needed an extra one hundred napkins, but really I just wanted an opportunity to talk to Mike. He mentioned something about not having anyone to go with him to the movies. My anger had dissipated at that point, and so I was able to say, with mock (but secretly real) exasperation:

"*I* would see a movie with you!"

I smiled as I said it, but he did not. I will never forget what he said, never forget his face as he said it:

"No. You're too good for a guy like me."

His grey eyes seemed especially dark as they locked with mine. They were heavy with sadness, and once he said that he looked away from me. Mike lacked his usual confidence and swagger.

"That's not true," I insisted.

Mike shook his head. "Yes, it is."

A customer came in and I went to join my sister and cousins.

o o o o o

Mysteriously, a few months later, I stopped seeing Mike in the pizzeria. I asked one of the other workers what happened, and he told me that Mike was fired. That night, whether it was the right or wrong choice, I called Mike. According to him, he quit, he was not fired. It was all good – he was on to bigger and better things. What those bigger and better things were, he did not say, but we talked for almost two hours and had a wonderful conversation. But it was the last time we would talk for a while.

o o o o o

I still found myself missing Mike a month later, so I came up with some contrived excuse to text him. I forget exactly what it was, probably something about the pizzeria – maybe an anecdote about his old, crotchety boss. He quickly replied once, then again, telling me that he missed me. I told him I missed him, too. He asked me what I missed about him, and having absolutely no idea what to say, I just asked him what he missed about me. Coy, I know. He answered:

"Everything."

I never loved looking at my hot pink Razor flip phone more. I told him I missed everything about him, too, and a couple of texts later I found myself making plans with Mike to see the latest horror movie out at the time. It was something about a psycho killer who turned into a gingerbread man or a swan at dawn. Or did he turn into a pumpkin? No, that's Cinderella. Well, whatever it was, I was just so excited to be seeing the transformative murderer movie with Mike.

I was also incredibly nervous: once stood up, twice panicked about being stood up again. To avoid such colossal embarrassment, and also to ensure that I'd definitely get to watch the slasher flick I'd been dying to see, I made my sister and her friend come with me. Because that's not sad at all, right? In the event Mike didn't show, no harm, no foul, and we could all walk into the theatre and watch the movie. If Mike did show, well, then what a coincidence that my sister and her friend decided to see the same movie! Unfortunately, the former happened. Mike never came. I watched the movie without him, a gnawing heaviness in my heart, feeling some sort of way that allowed me to relate to the crooked and crazed killer. Who was I to judge him? Maybe he had his own Mike, some love thug named Samantha who played with his demented heart one too many times before he snapped. I, of course, would never turn to murder like he did. I'm more of an emotional eater, something that came into play as I returned to the concession stand three times throughout the duration of the movie. I murdered about three thousand peanut M&M's. In my mouth. When the movie was over, I checked my phone, hoping to find some sort of explanation text from him, but there was nothing. I had never hated looking at my hot pink Razor phone more. I went home and cried and cried and cried, and I promised myself, that no matter what, I would never wait for him at the movies again. I was not going to text him, talk to him, think of him – nothing. I was done with Mike... forever.

o   o   o   o   o

Years later, my anger mellowed, my sadness evaporated, and my grudge went away. Not too long ago, on a bored morning at Starbucks, I searched Mike's name on Facebook. I couldn't believe when he popped up. He hadn't changed a bit. I swallowed my coffee, said what the hell, and friend requested him. Because really, why not? We live in the digital age, don't we? Everyone is Facebook friends with everyone. I'm Facebook friends with my high school teacher's pet dog.

A few minutes passed, and Mike accepted my friend request. He then must have looked through every one of my photos because he commented on one of the first pictures I ever posted on my profile. I was secretly thrilled to know he was interested enough to internet-stalk me. Not that I was about to invite him to another movie. I kept my promise to myself in that regard. But I did wish him a happy birthday and he thanked me and called me sweetheart. And on the most recent album of pictures I posted, he liked both the album and every single picture in it, which is more than I can say for some of my so-called "besties." A few months after that he posted a status:

"Finally released. I'M BACK BITCHES!!!!!!!!!"

He was referring to prison. He's back from prison.

So while I'll never know exactly what happened between

us – or, rather, what didn't happen between us, and why it didn't happen – I take comfort in our friendly social media interactions and the fact that he's out of the big house. I realize that long-term, Mike was not my Prince Charming. The shoe did not fit. But supposedly, there are many other glass slippers to try on. Supposedly.

Demetrius

I WILL BE CANDID: I HAVE NEVER particularly liked sports. I don't watch sports for fun. In fact, my favorite part of sporting events is the "kiss cam," and even that just makes me sad most times because I never have a boyfriend to kiss. So yeah, sports aren't really my thing. You know what is my thing? Sports players. I am a fan of athletes. Yes. Oh, yes. I watch *them* for fun sometimes. Their chiseled abdominal muscles, rough-and-tumble sexiness, toned physiques... and the sweat. Oh, the sweet sweat and enchanting pheromones. There's something undeniably attractive about athletes.

Especially the near perfect, neigh, completely perfect, athletes that we meet in television. You know the ones. Supposed "high school" or "college" athletes, the stars of their schools, played by gorgeous, sculpted actors in their late twenties. These athletes are tall, brooding, sexy, strong, and handsome, with a sensitive side. I mean, really, most of them are the epitome of perfection, and I could name one or two in particular who were the boys of my fifteen-year-old-girl dreams (I'm looking at you, Nathan and Lucas Scott from *One Tree Hill*). But, seeing as they existed solely in my television and the occasional wondrous dream, I never expected that I would meet one of these boys – or should I say men – in real life. That is, until I met Demetrius.

Some men are athletes. Some men are bad boys. Some men are European gods. Demetrius is all of the above. If you put a muscular athlete, a rugged bad boy, and a gorgeous European god in a blender, and then pour that mixture into a nice tall glass, you've got yourself one Demetrius. And, oh, how lucky you are.

I encountered Demetrius in French class in college. It met three days a week, early in the morning. I had heard rumors about the French classes being filled with hot potatoes, but I was careful not to get my hopes up. Sure enough, there I was on the first day, sitting in a classroom filled with eight other girls and five gorgeous gay boys. I knew they were gay by their polished, trendy wardrobes and impeccable hygiene. Those boys were just too beautiful to be straight. They were also all talking about their weekend escapades at the gay bar that just opened near campus. With two minutes until the start of class, I had resigned myself to another single semester when the door was pushed open with great force. In walked a male figure, quite literally tall, dark, and handsome. I had never seen taller a man in my life. I later learned he was 6'11, to be exact. Wowza. He was wearing our school's basketball team logo sweatpants and an oversized hoodie that I instantly fantasized about cuddling in. From his ensemble alone, I determined two things: one, he was on the basketball team (which made sense, because he appeared to be the tallest man on Earth), and two, damn, he wore sweatpants better than anyone else I'd ever known.

A few minutes later, as we were doing those unbearable icebreaker exercises, I found out a little bit more about the sexy giant man. His name was Demetrius, and he was Greek. But not just kind of Greek, like how some people say, "Oh, I'm one-fifth Indonesian and one-eighth Italian and two-thirds Swedish," but technically they've lived in America their entire lives, where they were born and raised and will probably die. No, Demetrius was *Greek*. One hundred and ten percent. Born, raised, and would've been living there if he hadn't received a scholarship to play basketball here. He certainly looked Greek, with tan olive skin, shimmering hazel eyes, and divine dark hair, cut short. He spoke with a thick, Greek accent that oozed sex. I had never seen such an exotic man in my life. He was like a beautiful figment of my imagination. Because he seemed so unreal to me, so out of reach, I was completely flabbergasted in the following ten minutes when I introduced myself to the class, and made some sort of joke. I heard a deep laughter in the corner of the room, where Demetrius was sitting, and my heart swelled. Did he really just laugh at my joke? Is this real life? A few minutes later, wanting to glance in wonder at the magnificent source of laughter, I looked over at his seat, only to find him staring in my direction, at me. But no, I was certain I'd been mistaken. I actually, as they do in over-acted movies and TV shows, looked behind me to find the girl he was *really* looking at. Probably a fellow Mediterranean beauty hailing from a falafel capital of the world. However, when I looked behind me, I found no more than an empty seat. So unless he was having a telekinetic conversation with an imaginary friend, Demetrius really was looking at me. I could feel my heart skip a beat and my cheeks blush. Here's hoping he didn't notice.

In the couple of classes that followed, it was clear that Demetrius and I were the star students. I'm not trying to brag, it's just a fact. We were the only two to ever consistently participate. Also, I'm pretty sure Demetrius was already completely fluent in French because he spoke with an ease and fluidity that I envied. I took French throughout high school, but my French accent lacked the pizzazz and authenticity that Demetrius's possessed. Probably because, you know, I didn't grow up taking weekend vacations to Paris. Anyway, as we were the only two students talking in the class, we developed a sort of interaction in that way. We'd converse in French beaucoup, and he continued to laugh at my jokes when I decided to share them. I caught him smiling at me several times and watching me as I walked back to my seat after writing on the blackboard. Receiving that kind of attention from him was exciting, and made me feel like Brooke or Peyton on *One Tree Hill*. Suddenly, I seemed to be the pretty girl that the hot, cool, athlete took a shine to. It was a role I very much enjoyed.

o o o o o

I had a bit of a routine established each morning before class. I would get to school about an hour early, go to the Starbucks across the street for my morning chai tea latte and slice of iced lemon pound cake, and then head to the study lounge near my French classroom, where I would sit at the same table every day to eat my breakfast and study. One morning, about two weeks into the semester, I was sitting at my table, minding my own business, when Demetrius walked in, spotted me, and then took the seat across from me at my table. I was slightly shocked, and very excited.

"Morning," he greeted, before taking a sip from his coffee.

"Morning," I replied, smiling, but not too wide or anything, trying to act casual. Breezy.

"Did you do the homework?" he asked, in his melodic Grecian accent. Homework never sounded so sexy. He probably could've said "garbage trucks filled with fish carcasses" and it would have sounded irresistible.

"Yeah," I answered (I always did my homework).

"I didn't," he grinned.

"You can look at mine if you want," I offered, my good-girl image flying out the window. He promptly got out of his seat, notebook in hand, and occupied the space right next to me. He leaned in close and I tried not to pass out as I gestured towards the open page of my One Direction notebook. He rolled up his sleeves before writing, revealing two tattoos. One was on his wrist – a Chi Ro symbol, in red – and the other one was on his inner forearm – a Greek word I clearly had no idea how to interpret. I complimented his tattoos, without mentioning how sexy I found them. He smiled, bringing his arms even closer to me for inspection. He told me that the Greek word was in fact his brother's name. He got it so that even though they were almost a world away, he could always keep him close. I swooned. I can't remember whether or not I touched his arm where the tattoo was, but I like to believe that I did. How bold, how sexy, how start-of-a-romance-novel. But after that moment ended, he went back to copying my work. We sat in silence for a bit, when he reached towards my slice of iced lemon pound cake, and picked a part off to pop in his mouth: the icing part, no less.

"Hey!" I laughed, gently shoving him. "What are you doing? That's my favorite part!"

I'm very territorial when it comes to dessert.

"So?" he asked with a mouthful of pound cake.

"So, that's the only part I eat anyways."

"You only eat the frosting part? Really?"

"Yes, really, is that so hard to believe?"

Demetrius laughed. "No. You're funny. A funny girl." I wasn't sure whether to be charmed or offended with his last comment. But before I could decide, he closed his books and said, "C'mon funny girl, let's go to class."

That morning, in class, when the professor told us to partner up, Demetrius came and found me. We spent most of the class giggling, with him whispering to me about his life in Greece and his family, and how much he missed them and his home. He had two beautiful homes in Greece, and he was counting down the days until school was finished and he could go home for the summer. I teased that he would have to send me a postcard. He smiled and said that he'd find me the best postcard Greece had to offer. As he spoke to me in a hushed, low voice, I couldn't help but revel in the fact that I was having an amazing and interesting conversation with a gorgeous, smokin' hot, Greek basketball player. Like, it was the stuff of dreams, to be honest... the way things played out in the movies, and I was living it in my real world life!

The next day, I was sitting at my table but had been running a little late that morning so I chose to forego my Starbucks stop. I just sat down at my usual table and opened my books when Demetrius walked in and sat down next to me. He pulled out a piece of iced lemon pound cake from a Starbucks paper bag, broke it apart so that the icing top and iceless bottom were separate, and handed me the iced piece. I was so happily surprised by the sweet gesture. I smiled and thanked him and he nodded, and then we proceeded to talk about our favorite superhero flicks. I inevitably started gushing about Wolverine, which he seemed to respect. We both wanted to see the new Wolverine movie. I mentioned that there was going to be an advanced screening of it the next day in the city.

"That would be fun to go to," he mumbled, looking down at his pound cake.

I paused... was that a hint? I couldn't even really hear what he said between the mumbling and the thick accent. So I just agreed, to be on the safe side. But it got me thinking: was Demetrius going to ask me out? He seemed to like me, and we shared plenty of flirtatious interactions. Now this last Wolverine innuendo seemed like a hint in the right direction, so why not? Him asking me out on a date seemed like the next natural step in our relationship. Oh my God, I was going to be the girlfriend of a sexy, Greek basketball player! I guess French really is the language of love. Or should I say la langue de l'amour?

And yet, another week came and went, and there was no date invitation from Demetrius. We settled into a bit of a routine in the morning, continuing to share a slice of iced lemon pound cake and then talk about either class, or superheroes, or his basketball schedule, or how he couldn't wait to go home to Greece so he could be waited on hand and foot by lots of women. Yeah, that last one wasn't so great. It was a bit of a bright, screaming red, chauvinistic flag. For a moment, it had me wondering if he even liked me at all, or just thought of me as a friend. But he was too flirty to be just a friend. So what was the hold up? Why wasn't he asking me out? I needed some answers. I needed some help. So

I decided to employ my secret weapon.

My secret weapon was my fabulous makeup artist, Ernesto. At the time, he worked at the makeup counter at a department store nearby. He created the most beautiful looks for my sister and me for proms, weddings, and other fanciful occasions. Plus, he was more than just a makeup artist to us; he was a friend and trusted confident. He also loved to gossip, especially about boys, so I knew he would be ready and willing to help with the problem at hand.

"Okay, so we gotta give you a look that is natural enough for class, but also sexy enough so it says, yes, I see you!" he decided in his spectacular Spanish accent, as he started working his magic.

When I finished telling him about Demetrius, his advice was simple. "Sweetie, you have to own that room when you walk into it. Because you're a beautiful girl, and he sees that. So have confidence and walk up to him, and you know, touch his arms, and just say, 'I like your muscles,' but very sexy like, you know?"

I nodded like I knew, but I didn't.

On the first day of class the following week, I did my best to replicate Ernesto's makeup exactly. When I showed up, and approached our table, I saw Demetrius look up, and then do a double-take at me. My soul rejoiced when I realized that I had just experienced one of those slow motion movie makeover scenes. You know, where the girl walks into a room looking all gorgeous and super fly, and the guy she likes does a double-take in surprise and interest, marveling at her beauty and realizing that she's what he's been missing his entire life. I mean, not that I ever went to class looking like a sewer gremlin. I always tried to look pretty because of my Demetrius crush. But Ernesto is an artist, and he was able to take my "casual for class but still cute" look to a whole new level.

Unfortunately, Ernesto's makeup worked no further magic. Shocking, right? It always seems to work in cinema. Demetrius still didn't ask me out, though we continued to flirt and developed an inside joke about rap music, and he continued to promise to send me a postcard from Greece over the summer.

o o o o o

Midterms week was a stressful time, and my routine with Demetrius suffered for it. He was a bit overwhelmed by the pressure of it all, because even though he acted like he didn't care about his grades, I knew he did. One morning, I was at our table alone, a little disappointed that he didn't come early as per usual. It was five minutes until class, and that's when I saw him walking down the stairs and into the room, only to pause briefly in front of our table.

"You." He pointed. "Next to me." He pointed back to himself. It was sexy. So cool and in control. Confident.

I got up, got next to him, and we walked to class. The next couple of mornings progressed similarly that week, though the gestures became wordless. He would come by our table with almost no time to spare before the beginning of class, catch my eye, and then nod his head in his own direction, and I'd walk with him. Yes, it was a little reminiscent of cave man days, but I didn't mind it. I found it sexy.

o o o o o

Things calmed down after midterms and Demetrius and I settled back into our old routine, but an unexpected twist kept me on my toes. He needed a link that our professor e-mailed to us a while ago, but he deleted. I told him I could send it to him – no problem.

"E-mail me," he smiled, writing down his e-mail on a slip of paper.

It was the closest we had gotten to exchanging numbers, and I cherished that scrap of paper. I only got more excited when I sent him the link, and he replied:

"Thank you! :)"

Yes, that's right. Exclamation point, followed by a smiley

face emoticon. I mean, could he be any more obvious? My cous-in, Desmond, once told me that when a boy adds a smiley face to a message, he means business. He came to flirt. So my hope for a romantic future with Demetrius was strengthened, my heart aflutter with the possibilities ahead.

But as soon as my hope was strengthened, it grew strained once again. *Iron Man 3* was coming out, and he and I had been talking for a while about how excited we were for its release. It was a day before the movie's debut, and Demetrius and I were sitting at our table, conversing.

"*Iron Man 3* comes out tomorrow," he said.

"I know," I answered.

"I'm so excited," he smiled.

"Me too," I smiled back.

You could cut the sexual tension with a machete.

"I really wanna see it," he answered.

"I really wanna see it, too."

"Yeah, I really wanna see it," he repeated.

"Yup, I really wanna see it, too," I said, because like, Deme-trius, if you are hinting that we should see it together, please just come right out and ask me.

"Wellthenweshouldgoseeit," he mumbled quickly, extra emphasis on the mumble.

I froze. Did he just say what I think he said? Or did he say that *I* should go see it? If so, way to be sassy, Demetrius.

Because I had no idea what the hell he said, and was caught slightly off-guard, I raised my eyebrows and incredulously asked:

"With *you?*"

He coughed and turned a little red, before shuffling around a bit and replying:

"Oh, well, I'm going with the basketball team so..."

Ugh, talk about awkward. I felt so stupid. I nodded, looking down at the floor. "Cool." I tried to act as nonchalant as possible.

To this day, I still have not seen *Iron Man 3*. Sorry, Robert Downey, Jr., but I'd rather not be reminded of my utter humiliation at the hands of a glorious Grecian god.

o   o   o   o   o

Finally, it was the last week of class. The clock was ticking, loudly. The metaphorical clock of love, that is. I really liked Demetrius. I was hoping that he liked me, too, and would ask for my number before our last class. It was my only hope at keeping in touch with him, a.k.a. dating him and taking romantic vacations to Greece with him and cheering him on at his games like any supportive girlfriend would.

I was at Starbucks one morning before class, catching a final coffee with my best friend, Ann, before she went home to Los Angeles for the summer. We were talking about Demetrius when he walked in. I promptly ceased my story and moved on to another topic. As he stood on line, I caught him staring at me, which of course made me feel like a beautiful sunflower. Once he had his coffee, he walked over to our table. I introduced him to Ann, but he didn't pay her much attention. He just looked at me.

"Let's go," he said, in that strong, sexy voice of his.

I gave Ann a hug before leaving with Demetrius. We walked side by side, our shoulders touching. Well, with his height, it was more like my shoulder touching his torso. Didn't matter to me; there was still touching. Almost instantly, I got a bunch of texts from Ann:

I quickly shut my phone so Demetrius didn't see, but I couldn't help but smile. Perhaps I wasn't a fool after all, if Ann could also sense the attraction between us.

Turns out, I was on a Demetrius roll that day. He and I walked into class, and Elle, the girl who usually sat next to me (my seat buddy – really nice – we talked a little in class, but our friendship didn't extend past the four walls of the classroom) wasn't in yet, so Demetrius sat next to me. We were talking and laughing, when Elle walked into the classroom. She pretended to be annoyed and tough, ordering Demetrius out of her seat.

He grinned, not budging. He looked at me. "What if I don't want to move?"

Elle stood firm, though, much to my chagrin, and Demetrius reluctantly got up, before flashing me that crooked smile of his that made me weak in the knees. So it was a good thing I was sitting. Then Elle resumed her normal spot, and immediately leaned in close to me.

"He likes you," she smiled.

I almost thought I heard her wrong.

"He likes you," she repeated.

"What?" I smiled, pretending to be relaxed while inside I was freaking the heck out. "How do you know that?"

"I just know," she smiled knowingly. "I'm so good when it comes to this sort of thing, I'm never wrong. He likes you."

"Oh my God, no. You think?" I asked, trying to be humble/modest but wanting more validation.

"Oh my God, yes, he likes you, he so likes you."

I never appreciated her more. Seat buddy of the century award goes straight to Elle.

After receiving encouragement from Ann and Elle, I went to my sister for advice on how to proceed moving forward. I knew she'd steer me in the right, normal, not creepy direction. We formed a plan. Following the final, Demetrius and I would walk out together, as we always did after class, and then, just as we were about to say goodbye, I'd give him my phone number, telling him that we should keep in touch over the summer. The plan was flawless. Or so I thought.

It was the day of the final, the time of reckoning. While we were at our table, studying with a few other people in our class, he brought up Greece. I smiled and reminded him of his promise to send me a postcard over the summer. He remembered, but said that he'd need my address.

"E-mail me," he smiled. "E-mail me."

I was excited. In a way, that already initiated the whole idea of keeping in touch. Maybe he'd even ask for my number himself after the final...

We went into the final and an unforeseen obstacle hindered my plan. There were two hours allotted to complete the exam. Demetrius finished within the hour. I tended to be a bit more thorough in my test taking, and when I saw him get up to leave, I was still in the middle of my essay: the largest part of the grade. I couldn't leave now. I wouldn't sacrifice my grade. At least I had the e-mail outstanding. I tried to comfort myself with that thought as I watched him out of the corner of my eye as he slung his backpack around his shoulder, and walked towards the door. Then, he was just gone.

o o o o o

I went home and regaled my sister with the semi-tragic end to my almost-love story with Demetrius. But then, we came up with an idea. I would look him up on Facebook and friend request him. Hopefully, he'd send me a message about needing my address for the postcard, or something like that. Hell, even if he didn't message me, I could message him without looking ridiculously desperate. That was better than e-mail anyway, I figured. What were the chances he'd be diligently checking his academic e-mail once school was out?

But again, I was met with a tiny obstacle when I found that his Facebook was set up so that I was unable to friend request him. The only thing Facebook seemingly allowed me to do was send him a message. And so I sent one, still thinking it was preferable to a school e-mail address. I typed out my address, and then, underneath it:

"I'll be waiting for my postcard :)"

Well, that was two years ago, and I'm still waiting for my postcard. I never received an answer to the message, never even got a friend request. To be honest, I don't even know if he saw the message, because I'm so afraid of seeing that little check – the read receipt – confirming that he saw it and ignored it, or forgot about me, or didn't care enough to follow through. So instead, I keep it collecting dust in my inbox. Because that way, there's still hope. There's still a chance that he truly never saw it. Or maybe there was a Facebook malfunction and he never even got it. And maybe he still thinks about me, every now and again, and wonders why I never e-mailed him my address. Maybe he thinks of me all the time, and checks his e-mail on the daily, like a maniac, still hoping for a message from me. I realize that the last option is highly unlikely, and that it's more likely that he saw my message and just never answered it. Thinking of that more realistic outcome stings. But, by keeping it there in my inbox, unchecked, I have no way to know for sure. I'd be lying if I said I didn't occasionally lay awake at night, restless and unable to sleep, wondering about the delivery of that fateful message. However, for my sanity, I think it's best left untouched, forever unknown, evermore a mystery.

Who knows? Maybe one of these days, I'll check my mail and find a postcard from Greece tucked in between bills and magazine subscriptions, from dear Demetrius, with love. Hey, a girl can dream.

Griffin

I NEVER THOUGHT THAT MY ENTHUSIASM for *The Vampire Diaries* would lead me to love. Unless, of course, I somehow met Paul Wesley or Ian Somerhalder at a fan convention and then we fell madly in love and got married and had lots of sex and babies. But the television show about romance and eternal life didn't otherwise seem a sure bet to nab a boyfriend. And I suppose ultimately, it wasn't. But, hey, it did bring me awfully close... yet again.

My love for the show itself may have petered out around the beginning of season three, but it led me to a tempestuous, exciting period of my life: a time I like to refer to as the coffee shop chronicles. Let me explain.

It all started when my favorite magazine released three different steamy covers featuring the stars of my beloved vampire soap opera. As a long-time subscriber, I received cover one out of three. It was fine, but not the one I wanted. I was looking for cover three out of three, portraying my favorite couple of the series tangled in silky bed sheets, consumed by their overwhelming passion for one another. So, I went to the nearest bookstore, hoping it would possess what I desired. However, it only carried covers one out of three and two out of three. I was not discouraged. My search continued. I went to another bookstore, but found the same products. My heart still hopeful, I proceeded to check all of the surrounding bookstores and convenience stores with no success. My positivity began to falter. Desperate, I turned to local grocery stores. Yet no one carried the elusive cover three out of three. Finding it became a bit of an obsession for me. I looked for it everywhere I went. When I took my sister to the oral surgeon to get her wisdom teeth removed, I scoured the waiting room, willing to accept Dr. Jenn's copy, even if it meant a few crinkled pages and a coffee stain or two. But it was nowhere to be found. I had just about given up hope that I'd ever lay my eyes on this coveted magazine cover.

Until one fateful, rainy Sunday morning when I decided to get out of bed early and get breakfast with my dad: the Sunday that would change my life in more ways than one. My dad wanted to go to Krazy for Koffee. By the name of it, you'd think it was a ghetto establishment selling some sort of knockoff coffee substitute, but it was real coffee. I think they were just trying to be clever with the name, or emulate provocative rappers or something. Krazy or not, according to my dad, they made the best pumpkin muffin in New Jersey, and that morning, he had a particular hankering for one. And who the hell am I to turn down a breakfast pastry?

As I entered the shop and shook the rain from my umbrella, I looked up straight ahead of me, and there it was: cover three out of three. Shining – nay, glistening – like a beacon of hope from its resting place in the magazine rack in front of the registers. I rushed to it, picked it up, and held it in my hands. I had found it.

"Hallelujah! It's here!" I exclaimed out loud, unable to help myself, not thinking anyone could hear me anyway.

That's when I heard a little chuckle.

Slightly mortified, I looked up to see that the source of the quiet chuckle was an intriguing male employee. He was standing behind the register, wearing the Krazy for Koffee uniform: black jeans and a white t-shirt with the bold "K4K" insignia gracing the left side of the shirt. He had curly, messy blond hair that fell slightly in his face in the most casual yet tantalizing way. He had strong but graceful features that gave him the appearance of a resplendent sculpture, carved from the hands of a gifted Italian artist, whose sole purpose was to convey man in its finest form. He was an inch or two taller than me, and slender, but the feature that called out to me the most was his eyes. They were a dark hazel, like two coffee beans watching me. How apropos considering our setting. What stood out even more than the color, though, was the kindness I saw in them. He had the kindest eyes I had ever gazed upon in a man. It was clear that his chuckle was not one of mockery, but appreciation. Appreciation for my cuteness and enthusiasm for immortal love, something I thought that boys should have been appreciating about me for a while.

To regain my composure as best as I could, I gave a sheepish laugh before pulling out my wallet to purchase my treasure. I looked at his nametag as he rang me up. In all capital letters, typed in thick, black boldface, was the name:

GRIFFIN.

Griffin. What an interesting name. Sort of... dangerous. Mysterious. I'd never known anyone in real life with the name. I had only heard of characters in the soap operas my great Aunt Gert watched with that name. As Griffin handed me my change, I smiled shyly and thanked him, still remotely embarrassed from before.

"Have a nice day," he smiled, his voice soft and calm.

That morning, I left Krazy for Koffee knowing that I had to see Griffin again.

o o o o o

A couple of days later, I returned to Krazy for Koffee looking my finest. I walked in, trying to be as casual as possible, nonchalantly looking around the store. I glanced – coolly – towards the registers to see Griffin looking at me, and my heart shimmied with the bold enthusiasm of a back-up dancer in a Broadway chorus line. He smiled when our eyes met, and gave me a small wave.

I tried to reciprocate with a cute wave, but isn't that one of the hardest things in the world? When you're so nervous but all you want to do is act effortlessly suave and sexy like the swagger-filled object of your affections just did? You want to match his carefree, gentle greeting without shaking or looking anxious or like you're thinking too much about it. You want your voice to sound low and sultry, not accidentally loud or unsteady. You want your wave or acknowledgment to be low-key but thoughtful. I always have the hardest time making it click. My voice never comes out right, my wave is always a little more spastic than I'd like, and I've never even attempted the head nod because I can only imagine how I would butcher that "chill" maneuver.

After attempting the cute wave, I ordered my hot beverage and headed to Griffin's register. He smiled as I approached him.

"He-llo," he greeted, with a musical lilt.

I would later learn that the melody in his voice with his greetings was reserved only for me. No other customer received the same sort of sing-songy aloha.

"Hello," I answered as calmly as possible while my insides did the Macarena.

"How are you?" Griffin asked.

"Good, how are you?"

"Good."

There was a slight pause as he rang me up.

"It's $3.09," he revealed.

I gave him my money. He gave me the appropriate change.

"Have a nice day," he said, looking right into my eyes and

smiling.

"You too," I smiled right back, before turning to leave. It wasn't much of an exchange, but it thrilled me.

o o o o o

For the next month, I found myself visiting Krazy for Koffee at least once a week, always hoping to see Griffin and share pleasantries. We never really graduated past our first exchange – it was clear that he was very shy and quiet. I'm normally not too shy, but my attraction to him made me nervous, and so the "hi, hello, how are you," remained our status quo conversation. Though by the end of that first month, I wanted more. I'm not the most patient of people, and my attraction to Griffin was only growing with time. Our short but sweet conversations were not going to be enough to sustain me anymore. It was time to come out of my Griffin-induced coma, and make something happen.

After my newfound determination to progress into more substantial conversations with Griffin, I was in the city, and spotted Channing Tatum running down the street. I don't want to brag, but we did share a moment of extraordinary eye contact. His eyes lingered. They totally did. It was one of my most A-List celebrity sightings. Later that same blessed day, I went to Krazy for Koffee for a soothing late night tea (a.k.a. to go see if Griffin was there), and was tickled to find Griffin standing behind the counter. He looked a little bored, but when he spotted me, his eyes brightened and he gave one of his perfect little waves.

After ordering my soothing beverage, I made a beeline for Griffin's register. He said his usual, "He-llo," and then I went straight into revealing my remarkable celebrity sighting with such enthusiasm and gusto that one would think the Channster and I locked eyes only moments ago in the Krazy for Koffee parking lot.

Griffin chuckled and asked for clarification on exactly who I saw. I repeated Channing Tatum's name, but Griffin still looked confused.

"Who's that again?" he asked. "What's he been in?"

My jaw dropped. I thought everyone knew *People Magazine*'s Sexiest Man Alive of 2013. I quickly listed some of his most popular work, which helped Griffin to vaguely recognize him. He chuckled a bit dubiously when I revealed our momentous eye contact, and I resented that because it absolutely happened. I'm not saying that Channing Tatum wants to marry me; I'm just saying that we shared a glance. I'm also not *not* saying that Channing Tatum wants to marry me.

After chuckling at my very real and truthful exchange with Channing Tatum, Griffin told me about the time he once went to a movie premiere in Los Angeles with his successful film-editor brother, and named all the celebrities he met there. While his experience clearly trumped mine – yes, even considering the eye contact – he talked in such a humble, quiet way. His sentences were short, almost cautious. Though he was certainly encouraging conversation, he was a man of few words. I could dig it. To me, it was still a great conversation, one in which I discovered that we shared a love for Los Angeles and movie premieres, though he actually attended the premieres in reality while I only attended them in my imagination. But still – it was common ground. Another wonderful thing about this conversation was that, since there wasn't a line of customers behind me, I felt comfortable staying and talking to him for a while. But eventually, I did leave, not wanting to be a bother or wear out my welcome. All in all, my mission to increase our communication was a success, and I liked Griffin more than ever.

From then on, our conversations covered a range of topics: the annoyance of allergies (his to peanuts and mine to pollen), close calls with death in the Krazy for Koffee parking lot, and our truest feelings about Justin Bieber. We had effectively broadened our conversation horizons.

Our conversations became more varied in subject matter, and consequently lengthier, but Griffin was still very quiet and reserved. I was the talker of the two of us, which was new to me, because before Griffin all the guys I liked were overzealous conversationalists. I found Griffin's shyness endearing though, and our interactions were the highlight of my week.

So much were they a bright yellow neon highlighter across the page of my life that I began frequenting Krazy for Koffee more and more. Once a week turned into twice a week which turned into three times week which turned into five days a week. There were some weeks when I went almost every day. I became such a Krazy for Koffee devotee: its most avid patron. I was quickly considered a treasured regular, with a VIP Kray Kray Koffee Rewards Kard and all. Please keep in mind that those cards were reserved exclusively for VIP customers, they were not just handed out. No, you had to earn your VIP Kray Kray Koffee Kard. I started my infatuation with Griffin as a girl who only occasionally indulged in coffee. A short while into it, I became a coffee addict. Lattes, mochas, black coffee, iced coffee – I tried it all. As this coffee addiction intensified, another addiction developed in me: an addiction to Griffin. Frequenting Krazy for Koffee to see him became an indispensible part of my routine. He made me feel so happy and exuberant. The way he looked at me was so sweet – like I was a cherished, delicate treasure placed before his humble register-space. It made me feel special. I also felt special because of our intimacy; it was clear that I was the only customer he exchanged more than two words with. And though his words were few, I appreciated each one spoken for me.

One afternoon, I went in for coffee and as he rang up my order, I complimented the pretty vase of flowers on the counter. Griffin sneakily plucked a red tulip from the arrangement and handed it to me.

"Our little secret," he smiled.

I beamed so intensely that I wouldn't be surprised if I had emitted rays of sunlight through my ears. I thanked him and walked outside. On the way to my car, I glanced through the Krazy for Koffee window and caught Griffin doing a little happy dance behind the register. Now, maybe it was his favorite song playing on the radio, but I have a hunch that it was our little flowery exchange that inspired the rhythm in him.

o o o o o

As time went by, I learned more about Griffin. He was humble and insecure. He didn't carry himself with confidence, though I don't know why not. He was a beautiful specimen of a human being. He was unassumingly funny. Whenever he cracked a joke, he did so in such a quiet way, but it was always hilarious. He was the consummate gentleman, polite and thoughtful. Even to some more tedious or trying customers, he never rolled his eyes or was rude. He was patient and respectful. And above all else, I think what I liked most about him was his kindness. It was something I'd seen in him since our very first encounter. One time, I stood in line behind a homeless lady. When it came time to pay, she pulled out a large plastic bag of pennies. As she reached into the bag to try and count the correct amount due, Griffin told her not to worry, and he paid for her food and beverage. Talk about having a beautiful soul.

o o o o o

Six months of coffee consumption had come and gone, and I was still waiting for Griffin to make some sort of a move on me. Not literally, like physically, move on top of me – though that would've been nice, too – but he hadn't asked for my number to move our relationship outside of Krazy for Koffee. I was frustrated. I liked him. He seemed to like me. Isn't that the secret sauce?

In almost all romantic situations, I find it personally preferable when the man is the pursuer. I know it's old-fashioned, but it seems less risky to me. However, these days, with the elusive and lazy and confusing men running rampant through the streets whilst captivating innocent hearts, that's a hard motto to stick to. Modern women must go after what – or who – we want.

I really, *really* liked Griffin. Our coffee shop encounters weren't enough to keep me satisfied anymore. I needed to see him outside of Krazy for Koffee. I wanted to go to the movies together, eat food (except peanuts) with him, and snuggle on the couch like two little squirrels. I wanted to touch him, beyond the slight graze of our hands as he gave me change out of a twenty. I wanted more. Six months was a long time for an impatient person like myself to hold on to something, especially something moving at such a glacial pace. But I felt it was up to me, whether I was going to go after love, or just let it stagnate. And I liked Griffin way too much to just let it stagnate.

Though I was resolute in my decision to be bold in the pursuit of something more with Griffin, I was unsure of exactly what to do. When you like someone so much, it's hard to be decisive about a plan of action. The stakes are high – you can't just willy-nilly do anything. What if "anything" doesn't work, and then you are rejected, and the person you like is turned off, wants nothing more to do with you, and leaves your life forever?! That would be a disaster on par with the world running out of milkshakes.

One brilliant summer day, I was in Krazy for Koffee, waiting on the ordering line. While I should have been staring at the menu, I was instead staring at Griffin from across the room. He was helping someone who had just purchased an obscene amount of iced chocolate beverages with lots of whipped cream and chocolate syrup. As I stared, I fell into a daze of sorts, imagining all the ways I could attempt to go further with the quiet, blond man of my dreams.

"Hey, would you wanna go out sometime?"

"We should hang out!"

"Sup, man. Wanna chill with me?"

"Would you like to go out with me?"

"Maybe we should see a movie together and then kiss."

"Are you free after work?"

"I would like you to be my boyfriend. How does that sound to you?"

"Here's my number. Please take it. Please call me. PLEASE."

"Okay, Griffin. Enough of these games. I like you. You like me. Let's just admit it and go eat pizza."

"Hi, do you want to date me and then eventually get married?"

Before I could conjure up any other possibilities, I had to order my beverage. Moments later, I was walking over to Griffin. His eyes looked happy as they watched me approach him. Just as I reached the register, one of my favorite songs by The Rolling Stones started playing over the Krazy for Koffee sound system. My excitement at hearing Mick Jagger's sexy voice could not be contained.

"I love this song!" I exclaimed.

"Me too," Griffin grinned. He paused a second. "There's this local band that plays in the center of town. They do an amazing cover of this song. Probably the next best thing to The Stones."

"Really?" I asked. The beans inside my head started bouncing. I recognized my opportunity. It was placed right in front of me. I was nervous, but I knew I'd hate myself if I let it slip away.

"We should go see them play sometime," I suggested. I was pleasantly surprised at how steady my voice sounded.

"Yeah," Griffin smiled.

Seeing his beautiful smile at the thought of us hanging out apart from Krazy for Koffee filled me with relief and excitement. Maybe this wasn't a disaster waiting to happen, after all.

"They play right in town?" I asked.

"Yeah, at Sullivan's."

"Oh, okay," I nodded.

"Can I have your number? So, we, with the show... "

Griffin turned bright red.

It was the best question I had ever been asked. I grabbed a napkin and a pen, and though my hand was trembling, I wrote down my cell phone number. Hopefully he didn't notice the nervous shaking of my hand. And if he did, hopefully he found it endearing.

"Thank you," he smiled as I handed him the Krazy for Koffee napkin containing my contact information.

"Yeah, so… " I trailed off smiling as I picked up my beverage. "I'll talk to you soon."

Griffin smiled and nodded as I walked towards the door.

But I didn't talk to him soon. A day went by with no call or text. Then three days. Then a week. After two weeks, I got the message. He wasn't going to call, and he wasn't going to text. I avoided Krazy for Koffee like the plague. I spent my time at home, in mourning, ironing and watching reruns of *The King of Queens*. In lieu of spray starch, I used my salty tears as they dripped onto the ironing board. My tears seemed to work just fine in ironing out the creases of my wrinkled clothes.

o o o o o

I stayed away from Krazy for Koffee for a whole month before I decided to show my face in there again. I felt that I couldn't avoid it forever. I wanted to show Griffin that his lack of a response wasn't going to make or break me. So I went into Krazy for Koffee. And I saw Griffin. And I ignored him. That's right. I up and ignored him. I didn't go to his register. I didn't say hello. I didn't smile at him. I didn't wave to him. I pretended like he wasn't even there. Because I can do bad all by myself. (I don't know what that means but it's empowering.) And the most satisfying thing about it, about doing bad all by myself, is that I could tell that it bothered him. Out of the corner of my eye, I saw him looking at me. Then Griffin, the most quiet man I'd ever met, was suddenly raising his voice as he did his usual exchange with customers, as if to get my attention and make me acknowledge that he was there. Well, sorry pal, if you wanted me to acknowledge your presence, maybe you should have texted me. You snooze, you lose. You don't text, you get reject-ed in person. I wish that last one worked better. I tried.

However, the satisfaction only lasted for so long. I kept ignoring him for the next two weeks, but it just made me feel worse. It was weird going in there and pretending like I didn't even know him, like I didn't even see he was there. It was also pretty out of character for me; I didn't like being distant. Ignoring him just didn't feel right.

I decided to put an end to our silence. It was the Fourth of July, and I went in to take advantage of the red, white, and blue coffee special. The look of blue coffee was slightly suspicious, but festive nonetheless. I had every intention of going to Griffin's register, but his line was so long, and the shop so crowded, that I was directed to another register. As I was leaving, I passed by his register. He was in the middle of a customer transaction, but he did a double take when he saw me looking over.

"Hi," he said, giving me a small smile.

"Hi," I replied, returning the smile.

From then on, things pretty much went back to normal. We fell easily back into our old routine. It was sort of torturous. I still liked him, and he still seemed to like me.

One time I was in Krazy for Koffee, and a rather charming British gentleman approached me to strike up a conversation. He appeared rich, well dressed, a little older than me, and noble – like an aristocrat. We were both on Griffin's line; Griffin was actually taking care of the man at the time, so he could hear and see everything happening. And he looked mad. The king/prince/duke offered to pay for my coffee, and Griffin's jaw clenched. I said thank you, but no, seeing as I was still waiting for my sister to join me with her order. He tipped his hat to me (literally, he was wearing a hat) and left. When it came time for Griffin to take care of my sister and me, he barely grunted a hello. He acted very miffed, not saying anything else throughout the remainder of the time. Little jealous there, Griffin? Well, if you like it then you better put a ring on it. Or at least text it a "hey."

But he didn't text me, and we just kept chugging along at our same pace. It was so frustrating, and when my fabulous friend, Teresa, came for a visit from Ireland, I decided to get her take on the situation.

"Facebook friend request him. Do it. That will at least bring the interactions outside of that damn coffee shop," she reasoned.

I was hesitant, worried to make a fool out of myself... again. What if he ignored it, deleted it, or thought I was creepy? I mean, we had a couple mutual friends, including other Krazy for Koffee employees I befriended in my quest to get closer to Griffin. They were, much to my chagrin, a lot easier to make a part of my life.

"Oh, please," Teresa scoffed, grabbing my laptop. "There. It's done."

"What?!" I yelled, literally falling off my bed. "Oh my God, this is horrible. Oh, God. Oh, God."

Damn you, Teresa!

"He accepted," she cut me off, grinning. "Almost instantly."

I jumped back on the bed, suddenly euphoric.

Teresa, you angel!

I swore I'd forever be grateful to Teresa, my own personal Cupid.

Unfortunately, Cupid's magic wore off rather quickly after the Facebook friend request success. We didn't interact on Facebook, and nothing changed in our face-to-face encounters. Admittedly, I was getting a little tired of it, my patience wearing thin. I still liked him, but in a much less all-consuming way. I think I was resigned to the fact that nothing was going to happen between us.

○ ○ ○ ○ ○

A week of Krazy for Koffee patronage went by, and I didn't see Griffin at all. Another week passed, and there was still no sign of him. By the third week of Griffin's absence, I knew something was up. Was he fired? Did he quit? Where was he? I was dying to know, but I didn't want to look like I cared, and ask someone who worked there. However, I realized that there was one employee I could trust: Monica.

Monica was my second-favorite Krazy for Koffee employee. In all of my trips there, she and I had become pretty close, often sharing fun small talk about the weather and boy bands and dessert. She also always gave me extra whipped cream on my beverages, so I had concrete evidence that she was a trustworthy person. I figured that I could try to get the scoop on Griffin's whereabouts from her.

"You know who I haven't seen around here in a while?" I asked Monica one particularly empty morning in Krazy for Koffee. "Griffin."

Monica's eyes widened. "Oh, yeah. He quit."

"What?" I feigned shock, but it was what I had suspected.

"Yup. Up and quit with no notice. Really got a bunch of people around here angry."

"Wow... do you know why he quit like that?" I asked, curiosity getting the best of me.

"Not really... from what I heard, he just like randomly decided to move to Vermont."

"What? Vermont?"

"Yeah. Go figure, right?"

"Wow." I was trying to process this new information. I wanted to know more, but I also didn't want to look overly curious. "Did he ever talk about moving to Vermont... does he have family there?" I paused a moment, before asking the question I *really* wanted to pose. "Maybe he has a girlfriend who lives there?"

Monica guffawed. "That's the funny thing. He doesn't have a girlfriend. We actually always thought he'd end up with you."

"What?" It was all I could manage. I was practically speechless. I wasn't even sure I had heard her right.

"Yeah. He liked you. A lot. We all kept telling him to ask you out. But he always said, 'I can't. I can't, I'm too nervous!' But yeah. We actually had a bet going on when you two would get together."

"Are you serious?" I couldn't believe what I was hearing. It was everything I had wanted to hear for so long... maybe from Griffin himself, instead of Monica, but hey, it was still something. I wanted to know more, still wondering if I was just daydreaming these answers. I had never told anybody in Krazy for Koffee how I felt about Griffin, not once.

"For sure. Hell to the yes. Every time you came in, he got so excited. He'd tell his friend, 'She's here! She's here!' We all thought you guys would end up together," Monica finished.

"Wow. I can't believe it. I had no idea," I replied, taking all of the information in.

I left Monica and Krazy for Koffee that day in a state of wonderment. It was surreal. Everything I felt, for so long, was just confirmed. He liked me. He really liked me. I knew it. I wasn't a fool! It was such an amazing feeling. It even lessened the blow that he moved to Vermont. I honestly didn't care. That much. Finding out that he liked me – that he wanted to ask me out but was too scared and that a whole passel full of coffee shop employees were rooting for us to get together – was validation enough.

Within the next week, another one of my Krazy for Koffee pals confirmed what Monica told me. It was a fun thing to hear twice. I was saddened by the sudden loss of Griffin from my life, but it was a contented sort of sad. Maybe knowing that he liked me was enough. Maybe I realized that I wouldn't have been properly equipped to handle his abrupt decision to move to Vermont. I like Ben & Jerry's but not that much. Who knows. But whatever it was, I was okay.

o o o o o

About a year ago, Griffin moved back from Vermont. He adopted three birds, had an antelope tattooed on his forearm, and dyed his hair bright blue. He looked like a little blueberry.

Last week, I was stuck in traffic while driving to meet one of my friends for dinner. I sat in my car, listening to the Ja Rule/Taylor Swift mix CD I made, when I noticed some guy in the dark green minivan ahead looking at me. I turned my gaze to the right, a little uncomfortable because I thought it was some old man member of the pervert parade leering at me from his decrepit car's window. I want a boyfriend, but I'm not *that* desperate. After a beat, I glanced back and decided to look the creep in the eye. Much to my surprise, I found that there was no pervert driving the van – no. Two dark, hazel, coffee beans were looking back at me. It was sweet Griffin behind the wheel. I didn't see much, except that his hair was back to its original blond color. He was a cute blueberry, but blond is a better look for him. He was still as handsome as ever, and as he watched me I realized how lucky I was that he caught me driving while I was looking nice en route to meet my friend for dinner instead of early in the morning on my drive to get my first coffee of the day, when I tend to look like a grumpy ghoul.

Before anything could happen, traffic started moving again. He made the next left turn, and looked back at me once more before I drove straight past him. For a nanosecond, I was tempted to turn left, and follow him. I didn't. I just kept on straight. But I couldn't help but wonder what I was driving past. What was I leaving behind on that left hand turn? A couple of possibilities twinkled in my mind. A slideshow of our potential story lit up the screen inside my mind, and I felt a twitch of longing for something I let go of a while ago.

But, the point is, I did drive on. I kept Griffin in the past. I kept our futures clear and separate. I think I'm happier because of it. At one point, Griffin was everything I wanted. But I don't long for him the same way I used to anymore. Now, he's simply a memory – a reflection in the side view mirror in the car ahead of me. It's a reflection that makes me happy, despite the less-than-fairytale ending I shared with it.

o o o o o

Griffin will always be a bit of a mystery to me, but right now, I've got other things to think about. There are more manly memories haunting me, and they aren't as quiet or calm as Griffin. These memories are loud, annoying, and won't shut up. There's one that's particularly irritating. One I just can't seem to leave behind – one I cannot drive straight past.

Sammy

We all have that one person in our lives. You know the one: when we remember being involved with him or her, we kind of just shake our heads and never stop asking ourselves, "what was I thinking?" There's also a lot of cringing involved because we'd rather pretend that it all just never happened. For me, that one person is Sammy. Sammy the Stock Boy.

I met Sammy the Stock Boy at Krazy for Koffee. He was, you guessed it, the stock boy. He also acted as part-time bus boy and would occasionally be seen sweeping the floors. On those days, he was Sammy the Sweeper.

I caught on pretty quickly that Sammy took a shine to me. He started saying hi to me and smiling a lot whenever he saw me. He was a bit bashful about it. He had this nervous tick: whenever he greeted me, he nodded a lot. He looked like a bobble head. A Krazy for Koffee bobble head. He became a little more brazen as time went on. If I sat down at a table with my coffee, to study or do work, Sammy would make his way with his mop to my table and try striking up a conversation with me. I say try because once it started, it was basically my responsibility to keep it going. Sammy was a simple guy, and didn't really have too much to talk about. There were three things he knew well: hunting, bowling, and Krazy for Koffee. He loved his job, and knew Krazy for Koffee inside and out. He could talk about it for hours. He also loved to hunt with his family, and was on a local bowling team, which played competitive games every Tuesday night and practiced four days a week. Those three things made up his life and were all he could ever talk about. Unfortunately, I did not share his same enthusiasm for those particular subjects. Unless he wanted to make a game of guessing what some celebrities', like Flavor Flav's or Ina Garten's, bowling scores might be. But otherwise, nada. There was just nothing scintillating about Sammy; nothing about him or his aura appealed to me. He was nice, but boring, and we had almost nothing in common. I loved movies – he rarely watched them. I was a television fanatic, obsessed with my favorite shows – he only kept up with professional bowling and *Family Guy*. I adored puppies – he preferred cats. I was Justin Bieber's truest fan – he hated him. Opposites are said to attract, but that just was not the case in this situation. Not on my part, at least. Sammy didn't seem perturbed at all by our differences. His attraction to me only seemed to increase with each new interaction we shared.

I didn't feel it, though. I mean, the attention was nice. It's always flattering when someone likes you, but I just couldn't reciprocate his feelings. No scorching hot chemistry burned my soul with desire for Sammy. There were no butterflies in my stomach or elsewhere. I felt no enchantment. My heart didn't beat extra fast as he swooped next to my seat with his trusty broom. He was nice. But you can't always get your heart to go ba-boom! ba-boom! on nice. There has to be that sizzle.

It wasn't even one of those situations where we had nothing emotionally in common, but the physical attraction was so overwhelming that I'd consider pursuing him just for the eventual tangling of our tongues. Sammy was attractive. He was nice-looking. Is it cliché to say that he wasn't my type? He was just my height and skinny. He had thick, red hair and dark blue eyes. A person who vaguely remembers the Jonas Brothers would probably mistake Sammy for Kevin Jonas, and just assume that Kevin Jonas decided to trade in his bass guitar for a bottle of red hair dye. Sammy was like the redheaded version of Kevin Jonas.

He may not have been my usual type, or my mindset's perfect match, but I didn't discourage Sammy's advances. I thought it would've been closed-minded of me to exclude him just because he wasn't my ultimate ideal of excellence in a male romantic partner. So I kept entertaining small talk with him when he approached me, even though it left me a little bored and was slightly painful at times. And when Sammy asked me for my number, after dropping a line that sounded very rehearsed and completely premeditated, I gave it to him. I figured I might as well give Sammy a chance. Maybe after a date or two, my lukewarm feelings would come to a rolling boil, and I'd be all like, "Sammy's the man!"

Sammy texted me almost immediately after I left Krazy for Koffee that day, and asked me if I'd like to see a movie with him on Friday. Knowing he didn't normally ever go to the movies, I was touched that he was trying to accommodate my interests. I said yes. Because why not? On the night of our date, Sammy was very chivalrous and considerate. He texted me when he was running a tad late, but assured me that he'd be at my house soon, smiley face emoticon. When he arrived, he rang the doorbell. I found him standing on my front porch, dressed in black pants with a silver chain hanging from the pocket, and a dark green, blue, and black plaid shirt. Not exactly my style, but he looked nice and smelled like a green meadow-flavored men's deodorant. As we drove to the movies in his bright red, severely scratched up car that was missing two windows, the polite conversation began. At first, I couldn't think of anything to say, so I said something about it being weird seeing him outside of Krazy for Koffee. Sammy replied:

"Yeah, it's better!" He turned and flashed me an eager smile.

Oh, okay. Maybe!

When we got to the movie theatre, there was an awkward moment buying the tickets. I didn't want to look like I just assumed that he'd pay, so I took out my wallet. He told me not to worry about it, I thanked him, and we moved on. I could tell he was nervous because he kept fidgeting a lot. I felt bad that he was nervous, but all the tiny movements were a little unnerving. They made it hard to relax. The twitches only worsened when we sat down in the theatre. Sammy immediately started rocking back and forth in his chair – his squeaky chair, no less. This rocking and subsequent squeaking was non-stop until the credits rolled. But before the credits rolled, and before the start of the movie, there was a little bit of downtime. More polite conversation to be had. Somehow I brought up my love for Disney movies, and he revealed that he had never seen a Disney movie. Not a single one. I was floored, as up until that point, I assumed that even Martians floating around in outer space watched Disney movies. Sammy smiled, and said:

"Well, now you have to show them to me. We'll have lots of time to watch all the Disney movies together now."

I was completely taken aback, and kind of uncomfortable by this grand declaration. It was only our first date. I mean, he must've thought it was going swimmingly to say something like that, but slow down, sparky Sammy! Chill, play it a little cool, employ some elusiveness. But it wasn't just the lack of mystery that made me uncomfortable. His statement constricted my chest into an oppressive knot. It was as though he cornered me, and locked me down. In his assumption of our upcoming abundant time together, it was like he was forcing me into something I didn't even know I had yet agreed to or wanted. I felt suffocated.

As we drove back to my house, his nervous twitches continued, and I wondered whether or not he was going to kiss me. During the movie, he didn't try holding my hand or feigning a yawn in order to stretch his arm around me, or anything of the sort. He just kept rocking back and forth. I was fine with it, though. I didn't even know if I wanted him to kiss me, because

I was so unsure of my feelings towards him. On the one hand, a kiss could intensify my feelings. He could be the world's greatest kisser and then, all of a sudden, I'd find myself incredibly attracted to him and eager to kiss him more and more. On the other hand, his kiss could be as boring as his personality and keep things the same between us. Then, of course, there was the possibility that he'd be a terrible kisser and a kiss would seal the bye-bye-Sammy deal.

He pulled into my driveway, and as he walked me to the door, he reminded me:

"We have to figure out when we're gonna start watching all those Disney movies."

His eyes were fixated on mine, as if I were his delicious prey. Sammy was the shark and I was the humble and defenseless guppy fish he was ready to force into a committed relationship. The musical score of *Jaws* hummed in my ears. The tightness in my chest returned. I forced a smile. As we walked up my front steps, I thanked him and told him I had fun. He agreed, bobbing his head all the while, and said we should do it again soon, as if reminding me twice about all the time we were going to share watching every Disney movie ever made wasn't clear enough. I nodded and then he leaned in to give me the oddest kiss I've ever had. I don't even know if I can call it a kiss. He put both of his arms around me, and then kissed only one side of my mouth. Like, his lips only touched a part of my lips, but mostly just my face. It was weird. And not very sexual at all. I've gotten better kisses from my dog. My grandmother's chaste kisses on the lips are more forthright than his. So to summarize, the "kiss" left me befuddled, and didn't point me in any one clear direction about how to proceed with Sammy.

All in all, I suppose it was a fine date. He was perfectly polite and chivalrous. He technically did all the right things. He even texted me later that same night to tell me that I should add him on Facebook, and then the next morning, to tell me again that he had a great time. I still felt that he wasn't doing anything wrong or outrageously offensive, and that he was a nice guy, so I accepted his invitation for a second date.

Our second date wasn't too different from our first; we went to another movie, he rocked back and forth in his chair a lot, and there was plenty of polite conversation that I think he mistook for engaging and dynamic banter. When he picked me up, he told me that he had a surprise for me. Sammy took out a plastic bag. Then, like a magician pulling a rabbit from a hat, he unveiled from that plastic bag a tiny Mickey Mouse stuffed animal. A nod, I suppose, to all the Disney movies we had yet to watch together. He clearly went out of his way, physically and financially, to get it for me, so I thanked him profusely and smiled widely. There was a bit of an awkward moment when we got out of the car; I went in for a hug to thank him, but he thought I was going in for a kiss, so we ended up bumping into each other with his face smushed against the side of mine.

I wish I could say that the stuffed animal gift charmed me. But it didn't. It made me feel anxious, like we were moving too fast. I was tormented, too, because I felt guilty that I wasn't swooning like a lovesick pup over his kind gestures. When my sister confirmed that it was a very sweet thing to do, I realized the problem. It wasn't what he was doing; it was that *he* was the one doing it. The lack of chemistry I felt between Sammy and me was what made his gestures disconcerting and a bit too forward, and that's where my guilt got me again.

Just because I didn't dreamily fantasize about Sammy as I drifted off to sleep at night didn't mean I had a good enough reason to reject him. It wasn't his fault that he wasn't Taye Diggs. I felt that I owed him a chance.

At the end of our second date, Sammy nervously bobbed all the way to my house, walked me to my door, and, this time, was a little more clear in his kiss: on the cheek. It was fine by me.

He called me the following week and asked if I would want to go to his house and watch television with him. I had no excuse, so I agreed.

His house — well, technically his parents' house — was small and kind of dirty. It looked and smelled as if nothing had moved or changed inside of it for years. When we first arrived, he sat down at his kitchen table. On it was a bowl of cheese doodles and an open container of almond milk. He promptly started eating the cheese doodles like they were going to disappear in a second. When he had his fill of the cheese doodles, he quenched his apparent thirst by chugging the open container of almond milk. Then, his cat walked in the room, which was bad on two different levels. The first being that I'm allergic to cats, and the second being that it revealed to me that Sammy was a cat-man. You know cat-ladies? Yes, well, Sammy was a cat-man. I didn't even know cat-men were a thing before I knew Sammy. He picked up his feline friend and immediately started gushing over him, stroking his fur, and staring down at him with adoration. Call me crazy, but a man speaking in a baby voice to an angry looking cat is not my idea of sexy.

A few minutes later, his mother barged through the front door, yelling about how she never had any "goddamn help in this goddamn house!" She paused when she noticed me, and scowled.

"Who are you?" she asked, seemingly perturbed by a stranger's presence in her house.

She only seemed more disturbed when I got up from the table to greet her with a hug. I have an incessant need to be liked, and also I hug everyone, so it was the natural, normal way for me to introduce myself. It was certainly not hers. Her arms stayed straight by her side as mine wrapped around her. I pulled back smiling, and told her my name.

"I'm Lorraine."

She did not return my smile. "How the hell do you two know each other?"

"Krazy for Koffee," Sammy answered while crunching on more cheese doodles.

"Customer or employee?" Sammy's mom looked at me.

"Customer," I answered, still smiling.

His mom grunted, her lips not twitching into even the slightest of smiles before she abruptly walked away from me and into a dark room.

Moments later, Sammy's dad meandered in through another room. He wore tiny glasses and a vacant expression in his eyes. I smiled and said hello, but he just stared at me... and he continued to stare at me for what felt like hours. Eventually, Sammy suggested that we go watch TV, and I was glad to escape his parents' presence. Though I wondered what awaited me during TV time. Perhaps it'd be when Sammy would finally make his move. It seemed only the natural progression of things, if we were going to be sitting on a couch together for a while.

However, this opportunity was quashed when I found that the "couch" consisted of two lawn chairs stationed in front of the television. We each sat down and started watching some cartoon show he loved. He laughed almost non-stop throughout it, and I started to count the hours until I could reasonably say that I had to go home. Suddenly, in the midst of the show, I heard the loud sounds of a trumpet blasting through a closed door adjacent to the room we were in.

I was so confused. It didn't seem normal, but Sammy barely blinked, so I didn't say anything. A few minutes later, I turned my head to find whom I assumed to be Sammy's grandma standing in the entrance of the room, staring at us. She was a tiny old lady, with white hair sticking up all over the place, and she wore a short, white nightgown. In her hands, she held a big, brass trumpet. I looked over at Sammy, who didn't even seem to notice her, so I just turned my attention back to the stupid cartoon.

Finally, after a couple of hours, I told Sammy I should probably get going, as I had an early morning ahead of me. As we walked down the stairs, I heard elevator music that department stores usually play around Christmastime – but it was the middle of September. As I walked further down the stairs, I caught a glimpse of Sammy's father and grandma, sitting side by side on the couch, staring blankly and silently at the wall in front of them. At least that gave reason to the music; I figured they were probably watching an early Christmas movie or commercial on television. I found myself mistaken when I walked into the room to say goodbye and saw that the wall they were staring at didn't hold a TV, just a framed needlepoint of a baby popping out of a watering can.

When Sammy dropped me back at home, he gave me two kisses on the cheek – slowly working his way to my lips, I guess. As he drove away, I couldn't help but wonder if I was being filmed for one of those hidden camera shows that evening at his house. Turns out, I wasn't. It was just a really bizarre night in the real world.

Strange as it was, I knew it would be unfair of me to hold Sammy's offbeat family and household against him, so the next week, when he told me that he was headed to the Laundromat and could use some company, I volunteered to be said company. I shouldn't have. It was the beginning of the end. It was the worst time I ever had with him, trumping even the night at his crazy house. It wasn't just boring – it was bad.

First of all, he picked me up that night looking pretty skanky. His clothes were dirty (which was probably why he was headed to the Laundromat), he looked like he needed a good shower, and he had this weird, crusty goo thing nestled in this eyelashes. Then, when we first arrived at the Laundromat, we ran into one of his friends, who leered at me a good bit before breaking out into a comedy routine, cracking sexist and racist jokes and praising prostitutes. Sammy didn't seem even slightly embarrassed by it. After his friend left, Sammy and I sat, for an hour and a half, waiting for his clothes to dry. We talked all the while. It was terrible. I saw a different side of Sammy that night. He droned on and on. He was incredibly arrogant and rude, and revealed that he had absolutely no ambition whatsoever. He told me how he dropped out of college without even finishing his first semester, because it bored him.

"Why would I go to school and be bored, when I could work at Krazy for Koffee?" he reasoned.

He continued to bash everything regarding education, ranting about how stupid and useless it was, knowing full well that I was in the middle of attending NYU myself and held academia in high regard. He proceeded to tell me that he wanted to keep his job at Krazy for Koffee forever. It was disrespectful, to say the least. Also, at a base level, I could not relate to his lack of ambition. My life goals were to work hard and make as much money as I could so that, one day, I would be able to buy a yacht and have bitchin' parties on it that 50 Cent would attend and also travel in the same vacation group tours as George Clooney and his lovely wife Amal.

As the dryer chugged along, so did Sammy. He continued to spout his beliefs about everything – the government, religion, celebrities, and popular culture. You name it, Sammy had an opinion on it. A very strong opinion, too. I disagreed with him on every account, but he spoke with such entitled authority that I didn't bother challenging him. I just wanted to go home. Or escape to Antarctica.

After what seemed like a lifetime, his laundry was finished and he took me home. He seemed perfectly happy, tickled in fact, as he pulled out a breath mint and tried to discreetly pop it in his mouth. I guess he felt that it was finally the perfect time to kiss me full on the lips. I had to hold back a loud, "Are you kidding me?" After the night I just experienced, there was no way I was letting him anywhere near my lips. As we drove, he told me how happy he was that five years ago he applied for a job at Krazy for Koffee, because it's how he met me. I was happy he had his eyes on the road, because I was too drained to offer a polite smile. When he pulled into my driveway and unbuckled his seatbelt, I told him that it was okay, I could walk myself to the door, but he insisted. I moved slightly ahead of him, swiftly towards the door. Towards salvation. When it came time to say goodbye, I quickly initiated a hug, jumped inside my house, and said goodnight. I was through giving Sammy chances.

o o o o o

Sammy continued to text me, as usual. I was polite, but distant. I even left some texts unanswered, hoping he'd get the hint. He didn't. When he asked me to hang out, I told him I was suffering from an allergy attack. When he asked me to hang out again, I said I had to help my friend pack for an African safari. He kept suggesting that we get together and persistently texting me. I was repeatedly being evasive and always circumventing talks of hanging out. But he never got the hint. Nothing discouraged him – not my late responses, my lack of smiley faces, nothing.

It started to get creepy on Christmas, when he sent me a selfie of him in a Santa hat. It was not cute or festive. At all. He was in a dark room, not smiling. His beady little eyes stared at me through my phone screen... watching me... haunting me. It was weird. I did not like it. I still sometimes have nightmares about it.

The next day, he texted me asking if I wanted to see a movie with him. I replied eight hours later saying maybe, but that I had a lot going on at the moment. He instantly answered, telling me all the days he had off from work, and asking what movies I wanted to see. I didn't answer. That didn't matter. He texted me the next day, inquiring if I thought of a movie I wanted to see. I apologized, but said I'd been too busy to think of it. Unfazed, he continued to text me, saying he couldn't wait to see me again. I didn't answer – I had nothing to say! I could have waited a very long time to see him again. Like ten zillion years.

But Sammy didn't give up. I was exasperated.

Then, Sammy sent me a Facebook message. He wrote that he tried texting me, but I didn't answer. He asked if I wanted to see a movie with him, and said that he hoped to hear from me and see me soon. A day passed, and I didn't answer, but guilt was eating away at me. I couldn't live with it; I'd never been so purposely rude to anyone in my life. I was developing a stomach ulcer. Or technically not because I ate a lot of brownies to cope with the stress. But I definitely had an emotional stomach ulcer. My mother told me to put an end to my madness and answer him. I knew she was right. I knew it was what I had to do.

I went on Facebook to answer his message when a status at the top of my newsfeed stopped me in my tracks: a Sammy status.

"I thought I couldn't be luckier to
meet someone so nice. I did everything I
could to make her happy, and treated
them like a queen, but I get ignored??
What a bitch. But it is what it is,
and in the end, its their loss!!! :)"

Sammy wrote a subliminal Facebook status about me, like a thirteen-year-old girl. A sub-status. And with poor grammar, no less! It was infuriating. How immature can you be, Sammy? Also, settle down, you weren't the perfect prince you seem to think you were.

I promptly sent him a message, saying that I saw his status, and that I was sorry. I didn't mean to ignore him (ehh), I was just super busy and overwhelmed between work and school (slight exaggeration). I finished with one more "sorry," apologizing that it took me so long to get back to him.

He replied in less than an hour, writing me a novella in return. He went on and on, lecturing me. Reprimanding me. I could picture him shaking his finger at me as he informed me that if I had time to log onto Facebook, I had time to send him a simple text. You see, he can be a sensitive guy at times, and he started to worry that I didn't care whether I ever saw him again or not. Well, at least he wasn't completely thickheaded: I didn't. He continued to bestow upon me permission to not answer his message. He instructed that work and school should come first, and that I should text him when I was free.

How was I supposed to want to spend time with him

after he wrote an obnoxious sub-status about me, something I wouldn't have even done in the eighth grade? And then, on top of that, he sends me a long, condescending Facebook message, instructing what I should and shouldn't do, as if he ever had the right or authority to do so?! You don't know my life, Sammy! And you're not my father! So stop being a butt and go bowl or something.

o o o o o

Thankfully, I didn't see Sammy around Krazy for Koffee for a while after that. Though I did receive a text from him, about a month later:

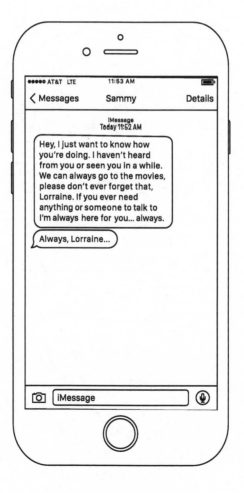

I didn't want another sassy sub-status about me, so I answered. But it was a little weird and made me feel slightly like an unstable person. I told him I was busy but good and asked how things were for him. He sent me two long paragraphs back about everything he'd been up to since we last spoke. Particularly that he got a job as a garbage man in my town. I wished him good luck at his new job, and that was the end of it.

○ ○ ○ ○ ○

From time to time, I still run into Sammy at Krazy for Koffee, and he smiles widely and nods his head a lot, and tells me all about his job as a garbage man. I'm always nice and polite, but I try to keep my distance. I suppose I'm still a little peeved about the Facebook punishment he gave me. And, also, the other day he told me he moved out of his parents' house and closer to mine, which was just the tiniest bit disconcerting.

Maybe I never should have given Sammy my number. Maybe I never should have accepted his invitation to the movies. Maybe I should have recognized early on that the feelings I had for him were never going to develop into an amazing, long-lasting love to stand the test of time. Or even a less momentous, but still fun, short-term relationship. But in the moment, I thought it was right to give it a try. I thought it was fair to give him a chance. It seemed healthy and positive to be open to a new experience and new possibilities.

I can't change what happened. As Sammy would say, it is what it is.

Scott

It was Christmastime. A wonderful time of year – some say the *most* wonderful time of year. Mariah Carey songs were filling the air with joyful melodies and the promise of Santa makin' the boys I desired mine just in time for the 25th.

My sister and I went to the mall to attend to some last minute Christmas shopping. We were perusing a display of *Star Wars* clothing for our father. A few seconds into said perusing, I noticed a well-dressed salesman walk right next to the display. He stood only a couple feet in front of me and continued to stand there, watching me, for the next several minutes.

I looked over at him, unsure as to whether I should have been flattered or disconcerted by the male employee's silent attention. The moment I took in his good looks and impeccable man-style, I decided to be flattered.

He smiled sheepishly, and I smiled back.

"Did you see the new movie?" he asked, shyly looking towards the stack of cinematic, sci-fi themed clothing.

"Not yet, but I'm dying to!" I replied.

"I'm going to look at shoes," my sister announced before

disappearing behind a clothes rack, leaving me alone with the attractive man.

We both sort of bashfully laughed once she was gone, but then quickly started a discussion on *Star Wars*. We talked about the new one, the prequels, the originals, plot lines, characters – being the only nerdy girl obsessed with *Star Wars* in my eighth grade class (even going so far as to have Jedi colored braces) finally paid off!

I bought my dad a shirt for Christmas, and the sexy salesman rang up my purchase, all the while talking about our mutual love of *Star Wars*. He ended our conversation by walking right up to me from behind his register to hand me the shopping bag.

"It was really fun talking to you. I'm Scott, by the way," he smiled.

"Yeah, it was. I'm Lorraine," I answered while trying to not turn into soup as we made some of the most fantastic eye contact I've ever had the pleasure of experiencing. It was so fresh, but intense. We were near strangers, so you'd think there'd be no depth behind it, but there was. Maybe it was the *Star Wars* bond, but I suppose it was more likely just a strong attraction.

I left, happy and exhilarated by the flirtation with a handsome stranger, but also a little frustrated. Why is it that things never work out in real life the way they do in television or movies? If that situation had taken place in a romantic comedy or half hour sitcom, things would have been different. Well, first of all, I suppose we would've been talking about something sexier, like biceps or leather. But second of all, and more importantly, instead of ending with nothing more than eye contact, our marvelous exchange would've ended with him asking for my number.

Romance never comes to me quite as easily as it does for the women in romantic comedies, though. I had nothing to report to my sister when I found her trying on boots. She was disappointed, too.

"I purposely left you two alone because he seemed to be

so into you! UGH, why doesn't life happen the way it does in T.V. shows?!"

It was something we lamented for the remainder of our time in the mall. We talked about how cute Scott was, and how he was such a good dresser. At a pit stop, while having both hot chocolate and regular non-liquid chocolate, my sister proposed an idea: why didn't I just give the guy my number?

It was an intriguing question, one with a million answers. Well, he could laugh in my face and call me an unattractive tree frog. He could wrinkle his nose in disgust at the prospect of holding my number in his hands. He could never call or text me, and an otherwise perfect and twinkling memory with an attractive male would be tainted with the sour punch of rejection, yet again.

But… this could be the one time that everything clicked, and it finally worked out. I could have a cute boy who was a snappy dresser to text and perhaps make out with and go see *Star Wars* with. And the fact that my sister thought I should do it all but solidified my decision. She's tough when it comes to matters of the heart. A boy could propose marriage to her and she would still doubt the validity of his feelings. So, a thumbs up from her regarding Scott was more than an approval – it was basically a guarantee. Oh, what the hell. I was never going to see him again anyways. I could do this. I could be a fierce, independent lady who went after exactly what she wanted with no fear or reservations!

Well, with not a lot of fear, at least.

Okay, so there was a lot of fear involved, but that doesn't take away from the fierce independence – it was still a baller move!

I wrote my name and number on a piece of a receipt, and walked with my sister towards his store. I was second-guessing my move up until the second I was standing in front of him at his register. He had just finished taking care of a customer, and turned to me.

"Hey!" he smiled, looking surprised and happy to see me.

Good sign, I thought. *Good sign.*

I summoned all the courage I could. I thought of how the risk of not giving him my number and missing out on great experiences with a seemingly great guy was bigger than giving it to him and not getting a call. I reflected on the musical lyrics of Fifth Harmony and Countess Luann de Lesseps.

Give me strength, Countess. And may I always remember that money can't buy me class.

"I just wanted to give you this," I smiled and handed him the folded up scrap of receipt. I was surprised at how cool I sounded, considering my heart was beating fiercely enough that I thought even the women at the make-up counter 500 feet away could hear it.

He took it, but looked sweetly confused, and I started walking away as quickly as I could without looking like I just found out that the zombie apocalypse was happening. I did not want to be there when he unfolded that piece of recycled tree and saw my name and number.

I knelt behind my car for about thirty seconds before standing up and regaining my composure. I couldn't believe that I did it! Once inside the car, I felt like such an empowered badass lady. My sister lauded me for my bravery, and said how impressed she was with my smoothness and baller diva move, kneeling in the parking lot afterwards notwithstanding. I reveled in the glow of being a baller diva, and tried to not think about the existence of my phone.

o o o o o

For the remainder of the day, I attempted to be cool about not receiving any calls or texts from an unidentified number. I reasoned that he was probably still busy at work and unable to text me, the beautiful girl he had instantly connected with at

Christmastime. Though I *did* receive numerous texts from my friends and Auntie Suzy. While I appreciated the love, each time my phone chimed, I jumped in excitement, thinking it was Scott, my new man friend and eventual lover.

Later, my sister and I went to the movies, and the entire time that my phone was on silent, nestled in my pocket, I bristled in anticipation. By the time the two-hour movie was finished, I pulled out my phone, almost certain that I'd have one, maybe even two, text messages waiting for me from Scott. Yet I pulled out my phone and illuminated it to find nothing but a picture of my dog staring back at me.

o o o o o

That night, I sat on the couch with my mom and sister, talking about the Scott situation. Why wasn't he calling me? Why wasn't he texting me? WHY DO THINGS NEVER WORK OUT?

"Lorraine, he's probably still at work!"

"At eight o'clock at night, mother?!" I was admittedly very dramatic in my time of frustration.

"Yes, holiday hours are later hours! And even if he's not at work, even if he just got home, what, you expect him to call you the exact second he's back?"

Just at that moment, my phone started ringing from way back in the kitchen, where it rested on the counter. All of our eyes simultaneously widened. We said nothing, all was silent but for the piercing ring of my cell phone.

It couldn't be ... could it?!

I walked to the kitchen and picked up my phone to find an unidentified number calling me.

Oh my God, this is it, this is him — things really do work out! Believe in your dreams, dance like nobody is watching!

"Hello?" I answered, nerves flickering through my body.

"Hi, Lorraine?" a manly voice answered.

HOLY HELL THIS IS EXCITING.

"Yes?"

"This is Phil calling from the computer repair store. I just wanted to let you know that your computer is ready for pick-up whenever is most convenient for you!"

I tried my best to not scream in frustration through the phone and shatter poor, innocent Phil's eardrums.

Scott never called or texted me. I've thought of a lot of reasons as to why not.

REASON #1   He had a girlfriend.

REASON #2   He lost the tiny scrap of a receipt that held my number on it during the hustle and bustle of helping customers with their holiday shopping.

REASON #3   He had a boyfriend.

REASON #4   He was moving to Alaska the next week.

REASON #5   He took a vow of chastity like the Jonas Brothers.

REASON #6   He was cursed by some voodoo priestess so that he could never call attractive women he had enchanting encounters with and find sexy happiness.

REASON #7   He wasn't attracted to me.

REASON #8   He got hit by a bus.

REASON #9   He is afraid of telephones.

REASON #10   He is actually a serial killer and
                 liked me too much to subject me
                 to his criminal lifestyle.

That last reason is actually kind of romantic if you think about it. Even if he wasn't a murderer, he could've been a pervert or a puppy hater. He could've even been one of those people who hate dessert. Maybe I dodged a dessert-hating pervert. Or maybe something cool with someone cute just didn't work out. Again.

It's okay. I'm not crying right now because I'm sad. I'm crying because I feel bad for people who dislike dessert.

Ashton

I'VE NEVER BEEN IN LOVE.

I've *thought* that I've been in love... I have mapped out at least three different weddings with three different guys whom I liked in the past. During those three times I felt very much infatuated with whoever was the groom-to-never-be. But I wasn't actually in love.

Every girl who has yet to experience love may not be able to say that she's had a love of her life, but almost everyone has had a crush of his or her life. The crush of your life, by definition, is the person you liked the most – ever. The crush of your life is the person you had the most fun with, who you clicked the most with, and with whom you shared the best, most electric chemistry. The crush of your life perhaps changed you in some way, or opened up your mind/heart/spirit in a way you didn't previously think possible. The crush of your life stayed a crush, and never developed into a serious relationship, hence not being able to be called the love of your life.

The crush of your life provides this wonderful and magical energy that fuels you with longing and desire and heartache and happiness and sadness all at the same time. The crush of your life is the person you think about when it's raining outside and you can't really explain it but you feel a certain longing. The crush of your life is the person you look for – on the street, in the supermarket – even when you know he or she is not there. The crush of your life is the person you think about every time you hear "that" song. The crush of your life is the person you emotionally return to, when there's no one new in your heart or on your mind. Whether you like it or not, the crush of your life stays with you. You'll like lots of other people. You'll love other people. But you'll never forget the crush of your life.

Ashton was the crush of my life. In terms of moving past the pre-official-relationship stage, I really thought he and I were going to make it. He was the closest of all calls. For a while with him, I really felt like I had found a partner. I felt that it wasn't going to be long before I'd be letting my inner circle (my family, friends, dog, mailman, etc.) know that I was one-half of an absolutely official boyfriend/girlfriend relationship. In fact, at the time, I was so certain of this official relationship destiny with Ashton, that I considered getting announcement cards for when it finally happened. Nothing tacky, you know, just a classy, 5x7 signature card stock announcement featuring his best photo to send to my close friends and family. I would have them read:

"It's finally happened! I have a boyfriend!"

Or maybe:

"The wait is over! A boy loves me! Thank you for your continued support!"

Something along those lines. I would've printed no more than fifty, tops. Maybe sixty. My family and friends would have been so overjoyed to receive them. My Aunt Laura might've even taken a picture of it and posted it to Facebook. Though the post might've been bad because I probably wouldn't have wanted the cards getting too much publicity. It would've been bad if he ever found out about them, you know, because then we probably would've broken up.

Ultimately, I didn't have to worry about any of that, because Ashton never became my boyfriend. Maybe I should have recognized much earlier than I did that it wasn't going to happen with Ashton. Perhaps if I'd picked up on some of the doubt-inducing signs that my friends were sensing, I could have spared myself a lot of heartbreak. But I didn't want to see any of those negative signs. I was happily entranced, under his charming spell, and I put absolutely no effort into attempting to free myself. See, I have this cute quirk (and by cute quirk I mean annoying character flaw) where when I like a guy, I am only capable of liking *that* guy. I completely fixate on him, and try to block out any other potential male suitors. It's like all the other men in the world turn into goldfish. Nobody else on the planet compares to my guy. Even though, in every situation, he's not *my* guy. He's just a regular, normal guy who is not in a romantic relationship with me. And no matter how many times people tell me to open my eyes to other possibilities, or hey, look at that cutie, or listen, I think so and so really likes you, it's almost impossible for me to hear them. I don't want to pay attention – I just keep my focus on my perfect, God's gift to the world guy.

It all started about a year ago. I was living full-time at my dad's house in the Hamptons for the winter. It was nice and quiet: perfect for writing and some "me time." By "me time" I mean re-watching the entire series of *One Tree Hill* with my sister while we were housebound because of a horrendous blizzard.

While many of my friends were back in New Jersey, I had a dear friend, Ashley, who lived not five minutes from me in the Hamptons. It was wonderful to be so close to her for so long, even though she did disturb my usual routine.

My snowflake emoji did not dissuade Ashley at all. I couldn't blame her. She had liked this guy, Shawn, for almost a year. They met through work, and Ashley was hopelessly smitten with him. She had found out through Facebook that his band was playing at a local bar, and her goal was to go and "casually" see Shawn and then have him "casually" realize that he was in love with her the whole time. It was a solid plan.

We walked into the dimly lit bar and Ashley promptly

moved towards the area where the band was setting up. Having been almost immediately abandoned, I wasn't sure of what to do with myself. I glanced over to the bar area, and was surprised to find a cute bartender drying a glass, looking at me.

When he noticed that I was looking back at him, he gave the smallest of smiles. He was so effortlessly and subtly sexy. Thank heavens for the feint and glowing light in the room, or else he would've seen how brightly red my cheeks turned under his smoldering gaze.

I tried to appear cool and confident as I crossed the room over to him. The entire time, his eyes never left mine. I felt like a revered celebrity. He watched me the way I can only assume I would've watched Rob Lowe if he walked into a room.

Finally, I was right in front of the hot bartender. He was leaning with both of his arms on the bar, still watching me. I couldn't help but glance at his perfectly toned arms peaking out from his black t-shirt. They weren't so sculpted that it looked like he spent all of his spare time at the gym pumping iron, but just strong enough that I'm sure all the hauling of crates of alcohol kept his arms perfectly tantalizing and buff.

But even more tantalizing than his arms were his eyes. One look at them up close and I was a goner. He had the most beautiful boy eyes I had ever seen. They were a brilliant, sparkling green color. When I looked into his eyes, it was like I was looking at two dazzling emeralds. They were stunning. Nay, penetrating.

Before I could get completely lost in his eyes, I managed to eek out:

"Hello."

"Hi," he smiled and used his amazing arms to push up off the bar. "What can I get you?"

"Martini, please."

"You got it."

His eyes finally left mine, only to fix my drink. "You're

here for the band?"

"Oh, no. Not really. Well, kind of... my friend knows the lead singer, so..."

"That explains it. Usually these guys don't get too big of a crowd."

"Are they any good?"

"They're not bad. Not exactly my taste but not bad. I just don't think too many people feel like leaving their houses in this weather."

"Tell me about it! I had plans to finish season 5 of *Lost* tonight. I miss my TV," I sighed dramatically. I was surprised at how instantly comfortable I felt talking to this super attractive man. He was easy to be with (and easy on the eyes).

"You watch *Lost?*" he asked.

"I love *Lost!*"

"Me too!"

He placed my drink in front of me. I asked him how much I owed him.

"Don't worry about it. It's on me," he smiled. "From one *Lost* fan to another."

I almost fell off my barstool.

"Thank you," I smiled, though I really wanted to say: "OH MY GOD really?? Thank you so much! This is fantastic! Should we kiss now or later?"

"I'm Ashton, by the way."

After I told him my name, Ashton started asking me more about myself. Before I knew it, an hour had passed, and I felt a tug on my arm, jostling my gaze from Ashton's beautiful green eyes.

"Let's go!" Ashley whispered.

"What? Why? The band hasn't even finished playing," I

reasoned, glancing over at Ashton who, I was thrilled to notice, was watching me interestedly. I didn't want to leave.

"Exactly. I wanna leave now, look mysterious," Ashley retorted.

"They're playing again next week. Same time," Ashton offered.

"Really?" Ashley at first looked surprised that the bartender was butting in on the conversation, but recovered quickly. "Awesome, thanks!"

"See you then, I guess," I smiled to Ashton as I got up to leave.

"I hope so," he smiled back.

I was lucky that Ashley was holding onto my arm, because between the drink and Ashton's overwhelming sex appeal, I'm sure I would've otherwise sunken onto the floor.

"What?!" Ashley squealed into my ear once we were a safe distance from the bar. "So he's super cute and super into you... "

Ashton was super cute. Of all the guys I've ever liked, Ashton comes the closest to looking like he could be in a handsome but badass boy band. He was about five feet, eleven inches: tall, but not too tall. He had short, well-styled blonde hair. Another person might say he used too much hair gel, but I say he used just enough hair gel. A man using styling product is nothing to turn a nose up to, if you ask me. Ashton had just enough facial hair so that it was a little scruffy and sexy, but not overwhelming and homeless. All in all, Ashton had the look of a totally, super fresh, hot and cute boy band member who did not live on the streets.

"This is perfect!" Ashley continued. "Now that you have cute bartender, you can come with me all the time to see Shawn play! And then, eventually, I'll date Shawn, and you'll date bartender, and we'll have amazing double dates!"

I loved Ashley's enthusiasm – and her plan. Once it seeped

into my brain, I couldn't think of anything else, or imagine any other outcome.

o o o o o

Over the next month, I went with Ashley every week to see Shawn's band play. And by "see Shawn's band play," I mean hang out at the bar with Ashton. He and I spent hours laughing and talking non-stop, about everything and anything. He and I got along so well; when we talked, it was effortless. Our conversations were the perfect combination of humor, flirtation, and intellectual stimulation. We had almost everything in common. For one thing, we had the exact same sense of humor and made each other laugh. This was one of the most wonderful things about Ashton, since I'd never been able to find a boy I gelled so well with, humor wise. Sense of humor is super important to me. It's probably number two (after number one: not a murderer) on my list of priorities in a man. So to find Ashton, a guy who also in the past gave someone a pillow with his face on it as a gift, was like finding a sparkling sapphire in a murky lagoon of goo and toxic waste. It was so much fun talking with him.

One night, he was making fun of me for always ordering the same drink.

"Don't you ever wanna switch it up?" he asked.

"I don't know! This is my drink, I know I like it, so I stick with it."

"Okay, well now I know what I have to do."

"What's that?"

"I am going to find you another drink that you'll like. I don't care if it takes all night. This is my bartender destiny," he announced with mock solemnity.

I laughed, and he then – true to his word – spent the rest of the night pouring me all different sorts of drinks. Some I liked, others tasted like poison. But I enjoyed every minute of it. Ashton did, too. I could tell by the way he looked at me. I loved it. He looked so happy to be there with me, and excited that we were talking. His eyes looked right into mine – he rarely broke eye contact. It was amazing and electrifying.

o o o o o

After one month's worth of Shawn concerts, Ashley was beyond excited to report that her efforts had paid off amazingly. She and Shawn were going on their first date. I was really, really, really, really happy for her... and also just the tiniest bit jealous. I wanted to be going on a date with Ashton. But I wasn't. And I didn't know why and it made me sad! Things were working out for Ashley, which was incredible, but I wanted things to work out for me, too! I wanted Ashton to chase me out into the cold air one night, and take me into his arms, and then declare:

"Lorraine, I've loved you from the first moment I laid eyes on you. All I want is to be with you."

And then, I don't know, maybe we would kiss and slow dance to Prince songs all night long and eat waffles the next morning, looking into each other's eyes with a bit of mischief and a lot of happiness, knowing we were at the start of something new and wonderful with a future of sharing many different types of breakfast foods together ahead of us.

"Maybe he just doesn't like me that way..." I thought out loud.

"Yeah, right," Ashley scoffed.

"I'm serious!"

"It's stupid obvious that he's crazy about you."

My natural instinct was to protest, but I couldn't. I did think that it was fairly obvious that Ashton and I liked each other. We were friends, but also more. There was a magnetic attraction between us that couldn't be denied. I felt it every time he looked at me. He looked at me like he didn't want to be looking at anyone else ever again... like I was all he ever wanted to look at anymore, and it made me feel beautiful and special. He also remembered everything I told him, whether it was that I had to replace the light bulb in my room or that I wanted to travel to Iceland. I once read an article that said if a guy remembers things that you tell him, it's a sign that he's romantically interested in you. So there you go.

"Why don't you just give him your number?" Ashley asked.

I could think of at least two distinct reasons why I didn't want to give Ashton my number, and they were named Griffin and Scott. After Scott, I'd sworn I would never give another boy my number again. It's scary. You don't want to be the one to make the move. But, more often than not, you make it anyways. Because maybe if you don't, you'll be missing out on a great guy. Maybe if you don't, he'll slip through your fingers and you'll be deprived of so many amazing experiences with him. Maybe if you don't, you're just letting him get away.

And so, motivated by such fear and my overwhelming feelings for Ashton, I did make the move. I put myself out there, and took a risk in the name of love and the pursuit of something more.

The next week, I went into the bar, summoning all of the "I'm a self-assured lady" courage that I could, and walked over to Ashton.

"Hey! It's my favorite customer," Ashton grinned at me with a twinkle in his eye.

I smiled, though my face was aching to break out into an expression of complete stress.

"I can't stay, I just…" I trailed off. I was holding a piece of paper in my hand. It was neatly folded. It had my number on it. For a second, I considered crumpling the paper into an unrecognizable, crinkled mess, and forgetting that I ever decided to do this in the first place. But he kept looking at me with those damn green eyes, and I knew this was something I had to do.

"This is for you," I finished, extending my arm with the

paper in it.

"For me?" Ashton smiled and looked excited.

I felt a flicker of electricity as our fingers touched, but the second the paper was in his hands, I turned to leave. My "I'm a self-assured lady" courage was fading fast.

o o o o o

Forty-eight hours passed after my brazen move in the name of love, and I heard no word from Ashton. Our fine affair was over before it even began. I was hanging out with my sister and our dog when my phone rang. My heart leapt, but as I walked to where my phone was buzzing, I forced myself to calm down. It was probably just a telemarketer. Or my long lost cousin's godmother or something.

I picked up my phone and saw that the caller was an unidentified local number. Internally, I couldn't help it: I was freaking out. Yet even as I answered the phone and brought it to my ear, I was still convinced that it was only going to be someone from some furniture company that my dad ordered a chaise lounge from that needed delivery.

"Hello?"

"Hey, you. It's Ash."

My eyes widened. I turned towards my sister, who took my look of utter shock as a good sign. She looked happily surprised, too.

"Oh, hey," I tried to sound as breezy as possible.

"What's going on?" he asked.

God, his voice sounded incredible over the phone.

I looked to my sister, who tried to charade to me what I should say. I knew I couldn't tell the truth, which was snuggling with my dog in my jammies.

"Not much... just got back from a party," I looked at the

time. It was ten o'clock at night. Did that even make sense?!

"Wanna go for a drive?" he asked. I could hear his sexy smile through the phone.

"Sure, that'd be great," I wanted to sound excited, but not *too* excited.

"Great, I'll pick you up in ten minutes. Just text me your address."

Ten minutes?! I immediately ran upstairs to change out of my threadbare sweatpants and try to look as sexy beautiful as possible. This was actually happening – I couldn't believe it!

Luckily, our house is a little hard to find, especially in the dark, and ten minutes turned into fifteen minutes. I used the extra time to try and look extra good.

He texted me when he arrived, and I walked outside to find his shiny black car parked in my driveway. I opened the passenger's side door and sat inside.

Ashton looked amazing. He wore a leather jacket and smelled like a rainstorm.

"You found me," I smiled.

"I did," he smiled right back. "You ready?"

"Yes. Where are we going?"

"I don't know. I figured we'd just drive… see where that takes us."

"Sounds good to me," I answered. It was so sexy I could barely stand it.

We drove around for two hours, even though it felt like fifteen minutes. Time flies when you're having sexy fun. He only decided to take me home when he realized he was running dangerously low on gas.

"I'll have to fuel up for the next time," he laughed.

Next time?! There was going to be a next time! Thank

you, spirits!

Ashton pulled into my driveway and shut off the car. He turned and looked at me. "This was great."

I nodded. "You're great."

I was mortified once I realized the words slipped out of my mouth. I started to say "you're right," but then decided to say, "it was great," and I ended up making an absolute fool of myself.

"I mean, you're right, this was great," I laughed nervously. "I meant to say... "

"So you don't think I'm great?" Ashton teased me.

"What? I... "

And then before I could figure out what to say next, Ashton leaned over from his side of the car and kissed me. I felt like I was in a movie, or a television show about sexy drama. It was the epitome of kissing perfection. I left Ashton that night on cloud eight billion.

o o o o o

Midnight drives became a tri-weekly tradition for Ashton and me. He'd pick me up after one of his shifts at the bar, and we'd drive around for hours. One time, I brought a mix CD for us to listen to in the car whilst we drove. We were in the middle of talking when my favorite One Direction song started to play.

Ashton stopped mid-sentence.

"Is this what I think it is?"

"I couldn't help myself... " I admitted, waiting to gauge his reaction.

He smiled, before turning the volume way up, and singing loudly along to all of the words.

I was in heaven. I almost couldn't believe it. I was driving in a car, with a man I was bananas attracted to... he liked me and I liked him back... he was a good kisser AND he was singing and dancing to one of my favorite songs by One Direction?! I was worried that I would soon have to bite my tongue to keep happy tears from streaming down my face.

Once the song was over, we proceeded to have a ten-minute debate about who was the best member in the band, and I floated up out of my body, watching myself discuss One Direction with a cute boy in wonderment.

Another night, I brought him a tiny box of my home-made peanut butter brownies.

"Thanks, Lo!" Ashton smiled. He always called me Lo, which I loved, since I'm such a sucker for nicknames.

He immediately opened the box, and took a bite out of a brownie.

"Oh my God. Babe, this is the best dessert I ever had!"

I didn't mind the pet names, either (babe, honey, bub)… keep them comin'.

He ate all of the brownies within five minutes, not leaving behind a single crumb. After such an enthusiastic response, and an affectionate "thank you," I brought Ashton many more brownies many times.

○ ○ ○ ○ ○

Two months into our driving dates, my sister started to ask questions, cracking what I thought was the perfect dynamic between Ashton and me.

"Why don't you guys ever go out, though? You always just drive around… " my sister questioned.

I had never thought of it that way. I guess I was just so crazy about Ashton that it didn't matter *how* we were spending our time together, I was just so happy *that* we were spending time together. But then I reasoned that if it was fun driving with him, it would certainly also be fun eating dinner with him in public at a restaurant where a bunch of people would witness us as a sexy power couple eating tuna melts or something sexier than tuna melts like sushi or pizza.

My sister also wondered why Ashton didn't follow me on any of my social media accounts. This I knew the answer to: he felt that he was too old for social media. He was 26 so I'm not entirely sure that I agreed with his feelings, but I wasn't going to argue with him. Though it did bum me out thinking ahead and realizing that meant I wouldn't get any social media love from him in the future. No picture of me captioned: "Wow look at this beauty, my queen, I'm the luckiest guy in the world how does this dime want anything to do with a guy like me???" Though I liked him so much, I was willing to sacrifice romantic-couple posts from him. If that was the only flaw he had, well, then I could've done a lot worse.

But I was interested in pursuing a date with Ashton that involved an activity other than driving. So, the next time we were on one of our late night drives, I decided to broach the idea. We had both talked about how much we loved sushi, so I saw that as my opportunity.

"Next time we hang out would you wanna get sushi? There's this great place in the center of town," I ever-so-casually suggested.

"What, are you getting tired of our drives?" he smiled at me sideways.

"No, I just thought it might be fun... "

"It would be fun," Ashton confirmed. "Just with my stu-pid work schedule I don't know when it could happen. Plus, I kinda like having you all to myself."

I smiled as he reached over and squeezed my hand. It wasn't a terrible situation to be in.

The next time we were on one of our drives, we were parked in front of a beach about twenty minutes from my house.

"So I felt bad about what you said the last time we hung out... that stupid work keeps us from having real dates. So I have a little surprise for you," Ashton grinned.

A surprise? For me? I got so excited. What would it be? Chocolates? Diamonds? Flowers? My mind raced with happy anticipation as Ashton got out of the car and retrieved something from the trunk. He returned to me with his guitar. He cleared his throat, gave a small smile, and then started playing an acoustic version of my favorite One Direction song. It was one of the sweetest, most thoughtful things a guy ever did for me. I loved every perfect, beautiful second of it. It was definitely better than diamonds, and even better than chocolate. I know that sounds crazy but it's true. The second he was finished playing the song, I jumped into his arms and kissed him senseless. How could I not? He was a guitar playing, rock and roll sex god. Ashton was good at everything.

Much to my delight, the surprise did not end with the musical performance. It was an unseasonably warm night in early spring. Ashton led me onto the beach, where he set up a picnic under the stars.

"So it's too late to actually go to the restaurant you like, but I snuck out of work for ten minutes and got take out before it closed," Ashton grinned and held up a bag containing all of our favorite sushi rolls.

Good thing I don't know how to do cartwheels, or else I don't think I would've been able to control my body from breaking out into twelve celebratory cartwheels around Ashton right then and there. It was the most romantic thing to ever happen to me. Ashton and I had the whole beach to ourselves. We stayed on the sand until the sun came up. It was sweet sushi paradise.

I didn't think nights as perfect as the one I experienced with Ashton on the beach existed outside of romance novels and movies. He more than made up for the lack of diversity in our dates. I was so, so happy with him.

o o o o o

Some time later, my sister and I were food shopping to

get fixings for dinner. We had just walked through the automatic doors and into the spacious grocery store, when I spotted Ashton perusing the produce section. Instantly, I brightened. As he was focused on a mountain of avocados, I tapped him on the shoulder.

"Hey you," I smiled.

Ashton's entire face paled when he turned to find me standing there. It was the complete opposite reaction I was used to receiving from him.

"Lorraine. Hi," he uttered.

Something was clearly wrong. I opened my mouth to say something when a girl walked right up to him.

"Babe, I didn't find coconut milk but I found coconut water is that okay?"

A dismal cloud of doom surrounded me where I stood next to the oranges. The happiness I had felt mere moments ago vanished. Despair instantly replaced it, seeping into every crevice of my body.

"Uh, sure," Ashton answered quickly.

The girl then questioningly looked at me.

"This is Lorraine. She's a customer at the bar."

The guy who I thought was a mere blink away from being my boyfriend was now referring to me as just a customer at the bar where he worked. After all the time we spent together, after everything we did, I was reduced to no more than an acquaintance in his life. I was in such a state of shock. I felt like I couldn't move.

After a beat, Ashton continued:

"This is my girlfriend, Dominique."

Before that moment, I never would've thought it possible to go from adoring someone to hating them so quickly. All at once, I was filled with sadness, confusion, anger, hatred, and desperation. I wanted to sink into the floor and disappear, reappearing in someplace beautiful and wonderful and far away from that damned supermarket. Someplace preferably also inhabited by Harry Styles and Chris Harrison and lots of pizza and puppies.

"Hi," I barely uttered to Dominique. "I should probably go find my sister, she disappeared on me!" I forced a smile before leaving to find her.

Suddenly, everything made sense: why we never went out, why we only drove around in the dead of night, why he really didn't have social media. Too old my butt. He just didn't want me seeing pictures of his girlfriend! I felt so betrayed, so embarrassed, and so foolish.

Somehow I managed to hold in my tears until we reached our house. Then, once in the privacy of my den, I sunk into our amazingly comfy couch and burst into tears. My sister hugged me close, and tried to comfort me. The next morning she even got up early to buy me a box of my favorite candy and a men's fitness magazine with Charlie Hunnam on the cover. It helped ever-so-slightly.

o o o o o

I have not spoken to Ashton since. He never reached out to me, and I never reached out to him. Sometimes I wish he would call me, just so I could ignore him. Then, other days, I wish he would text me, so I could reply with the perfect "to hell with you" speech. But he never has, and I don't think he ever will. I would hope that his soul isn't entirely black and at least sometimes he goes to dial my number; perhaps there's been even just one time that he began crafting an apology text, when he realized that he'd never be able to properly apologize to me, and so he sadly put his phone down and decided against it.

My primary emotion in dealing with the aftermath of Ashton was sadness. Eventually, my sadness gave way to anger, and I sporadically felt the urge to punch a pillow whenever I thought of him. Now, slowly but surely, I'm working my way to apathy. Whatever, right? Good riddance. You don't want me?

Well, maybe I don't want you. Yeah, how's that for a turn of events! Guess what, Ashton? I'm going to be okay. My world will keep turning even though you decided to be a human turd. I'll still have great friends and an amazing family and wonderful experiences and eventually, my feelings for you will disappear, like a pile of cookies put before me. I'm sure one day I will look back on our time together without an ache in my heart. Soon enough, I'll stop missing you and the moments we shared before it all went to the pits. Perhaps I'll find someone who's actually worth my time – a real man who dates me and only me and knows better than to act like a frightened skunk in a thunderstorm. My friend, Taylor, thinks that my perfect guy is an actor in his early thirties with chiseled abdominal muscles. Well, Taylor, I agree. Let's pursue this.

Anybody know of a single actor in his thirties, looking for a girl who enjoys Junior Mints, Tyler Perry movies, and long walks on the beach?

Conclusion

SO THERE YOU HAVE IT. MY PAST history with the most significant men of my life, all wrapped up and tied with a bow. A history filled with expectations, disappointments, excitement, lust, attraction, anger, sadness, happiness... pretty much the full spectrum of human emotion. I don't want to be dramatic, but it's taken a lot of mental and emotional stamina. It feels like I've been on a roller coaster ride, trekking through a dangerous jungle in Africa, flying an airplane in the middle of a hail storm, and watching *The Bachelorette* on repeat all at once. My nerves are shot. It's hard, living and loving.

Dredging up all of these old memories with all the men I've liked and lost caused me to re-experience all the emotions I felt with them at the time of our respective flirtations, both good and bad. Parts of it were fun and left me with a sort of nostalgia. It was mostly pretty painful, though, having to relive the disappointment. All the old frustrations and the unanswered questions came back – the pang of not knowing what might have or could have been.

That's the trillion-dollar question. What could have been? And why couldn't it? Why doesn't it work out with any of these guys?

Maybe everything happens for a reason. Even though I was sad that Mike and I never made it official, maybe if we had then eventually I would've been thrown in jail for being an accessory to some sort of crime he and his home-dogs committed. I was disappointed that things with Griffin never panned out, but maybe if they had, I would've stopped eating peanuts and dyed my hair neon blue and I'd be afraid to look at myself in the mirror. Perhaps if Demetrius and I dated, I would've had to start watching a lot of sports and therefore sacrifice my TV time with my favorite zombie fighters and Chris Harrison trying to help men and women find love by handing out flowers to each other. Maybe it never worked out for a reason. Maybe if I hadn't been single all this time I wouldn't be... me.

And so to all my fellow single ladies I say do not despair! We are who we are because of our singleness. We don't need boys to define us. We can let our interesting and dynamic lives and spirits speak for themselves. We are strong, independent, amazing women who don't need to rely on men for happiness and love!

That feels good for a while. I believe it, I know it, I feel it. I relish in my singledom, realizing that a boyfriend would keep me from focusing on just me. A boyfriend would take away precious quality time spent with friends and family. A boyfriend would take up too much of my energy. A boyfriend would keep me from flirting and hooking up with all the hot guys I meet when I'm out with my girls. I like being single, it's fun! I don't need a boyfriend, I'm going to make it on my own!

But then, sooner or later, the girl power fades. The reasons why having a boyfriend would be so cumbersome no longer seem convincing, and the reasons why life is lacking without one come into focus. A boyfriend would make me smile because he'd tell me I was cute when I did something silly. A boyfriend would kiss me and hug me all the livelong day. A boyfriend would hold my hand as we walked down a picturesque street one breezy summer night. A boyfriend would be my date to my friend's wedding and we'd slow dance to all the best songs. A boyfriend would give me his jacket when it's cold outside and I'm wearing a fashion-forward dress that doesn't protect me from the elements. I hate being single, it's not fun. Why the heck don't I have a boyfriend?

It's exasperating because I really don't have a good explanation for it. If anything, trying to figure it out makes me sad because I start to believe that there's something wrong with me. Perhaps I'm the reason nothing ever works out. All of these guys, who I liked so much, just must not have liked me enough to want more with me.

Am I not pretty enough? Hot enough? Smart enough, funny enough, cool enough, interesting enough... I start spiraling out of control, over-thinking every last detail about my personality and my physical appearance, trying to pinpoint just exactly how I am to blame for things not working out with the guys I like. What is it about me? What's my fatal flaw or flaws that prevent guys from wanting more with me?

But then I think, no. It's not me. It has got to be them. Because I'm not the only one suffering here. I'm surrounded by beautiful, sparkling single ladies who I don't think are lacking in any areas at all: my sister, Ann, Ashley, Taylor... and many, many more. Ann knew one guy for five years; they met in school. After graduation, she moved back home to Los Angeles and he moved to Texas for a job opportunity. She was absolutely crazy about him, and he seemed to reciprocate her feelings. He was always sending her pictures of things he saw in his day-to-day life that reminded him of her. They talked all the time, non-stop, via text, e-mail, telephone, and video chat. She sent him cards on his birthday and other holidays, and he sent her pictures of his fireplace mantle to show her they were perpetually on display. Last year, he moved to Los Angeles, and Ann and I were both so ecstatic when he asked her out for drinks. They went out, she looked gorgeous, and they stayed at the bar until it closed, kissing and talking in the cozy booth they occupied. They each left starry-eyed. But that was the end of it. They texted sporadically after that, but he never asked to see her again. Ashley was dating Shawn for a month. I had never seen her so incandescently happy. Everything between them was going splendidly. He even posted a picture of her wearing his favorite football player's jersey, and captioned it: "perfect." Then, at the end of that seemingly amazing month, she asked him to be her date at her cousin's wedding. He agreed, and Ashley was ecstatic that she'd be able to show off her hot, bearded boyfriend to her judgmental cousin. But her ecstasy turned to despair when, the next day, she got a text from Shawn, rescinding his agreement to be Ashley's wedding date. He told her that he wasn't ready for anything serious, and that he thought she was more invested in him than he was in her. He ended by saying that he hoped they could still be friends. They aren't. Poor Ashley still cries if Shawn's name is ever brought up.

The confusing and mind-boggling situations that we endure with members of the opposite sex seem to be ceaseless. The love gods apparently hate us. We must have brought pain upon their families in a past life.

But assuming we weren't terrible people to the kin of the love gods in previous lives, I remain perplexed and baffled. My friend Tara once "dated" a guy who she had to pay for all the time. She drove him everywhere – to work, even to and from the bar if he wanted to hang out with his buddies at an ungodly hour. She bought him presents galore – including courtside tickets to at least four basketball games – crafted him many homemade treasures, and cooked him his favorite meals whenever he asked. The entire time this was going on, he refused to say or admit that they were dating. He'd get annoyed, sometimes even angry, if she asked him to introduce her to people as his girlfriend. I don't get it. I didn't get it then, and I don't get it now. Why are there so many evasive men willing to let so many great girls elude them?

Because you know what? We are catches. Great ones, too, like big swordfishes or salmons. I love salmon. And it's a shame because the men are the ones missing out at the end of the day.

Because us girls that they left behind, the great big school of salmon? Well, we'd treat them right and buy them great birthday presents and "hey, this is just 'cause it's Tuesday" presents and make their lives exciting and interesting and all-around wondrous. We'd fill their worlds with amazing amounts of incomparable joy and love and fulfillment. And one of these days, they're going to realize that. Mike's going to realize it, Demetrius is going to realize it, Griffin's going to realize it, Ashton is going to realize it, and every other Nick, Juan, and Joe is going to realize it, but it will be too late and we'll have picked up and moved on, knowing that we are oh-so-worth it. We'll be happy and feel good and not let the opinions of smelly boys make or break our self-validation. Because we will know, without a flicker of doubt in our minds, that we are catches.

Then eventually, I'll find someone who loves me and wants to be with me. Someone who will laugh at my jokes, even if they're weird, because he gets me. Someone who will post pictures of me on the Internet and caption them "my queen." Someone who I can bake lots of cookies for and bring to my family's law office to meet my Auntie Suzy. Someone who will worry about me and think about me on the daily and call me darlin' and wink at me across a room full of people. Someone I can throw marshmallows at and play with in the ocean and eat pumpkin pancakes with at 7:00 a.m. on my birthday. Someone who will dance with me to Michael Jackson songs and carry heavy water bottles for me when I'm food shopping.

Maybe he's just around the corner. Maybe I'll meet him in a year. Maybe I'll bump into him in a month or a day or a week. Maybe we'll meet on an airplane or in a bar or at a post office or in San Diego. Maybe he'll have blonde hair and brown eyes or brown hair and blue eyes. Maybe he'll have rippling arm muscles and broad shoulders. Maybe he won't have any bulging muscles at all but he'll be super witty. Maybe he'll be really smart but afraid of spiders. Maybe he'll hate salads but have a lot of patience. Maybe he'll be very ambitious and a good listener. Maybe he will love football and volunteer at an old folks' home.

Maybe he will in fact be a member of One Direction. (Here's hopin'.)

I have to hold on to the hope that I *will* find someone. I have to believe that there's a guy out there for me. A swell guy who will be amazing and make me feel amazing. I deserve it. Because you know what?

I'm a catch.

Lorraine Cambria

Acknowledgements

TO MY PERFECT AND EXQUISITE RUBY
JEWEL OF A SISTER, CHRISTINA...

I've never known someone so beautiful, inside and out. This book would not be what it is today without you. I cannot thank you enough for your wisdom, creativity, patience, time, and expertise. Also, for reigning me in and telling me when I was referencing One Direction "too much." I adore you so completely. Dela.

TO MY INCOMPARABLE MOTHER...

You are the Beverly Goldberg to my Barry Goldberg. Thank you for every question answered (some a million times over), for entertaining my every thought, and for supporting me endlessly and unfailingly. You gave me the courage to do this. Thank you for inspiring me and loving me. You are a woman to love!

TO MY DAD, THE SMARTEST MAN I KNOW...

Thank you for your unfailing wisdom, knowledge, and advice. Thank you for getting me One Direction concert tickets.

Thank you for being a wonderful example of how a man should be. Thank you for being my "TWD" buddy. Thank you for always making me feel loved. Thank you for being "the man."

TO DAVID MY TALENTED AND MAGNIFICENT GRAPHIC DESIGNER PRINCE OF A COUSIN...

Thank you for helping this dream of mine come true with your masterful skill. All the way from Belgium and India, you took the time to exceed my expectations with a phenomenal book design. Your skill, craft, and genius are more valuable to me than a lock of Chris Harrison's hair.

TO BEAUTIFUL BRITTANY, THE BEST FRIEND AND RELATIONSHIP ADVISOR A GIRL COULD ASK FOR...

Thank you for all of the endless discussions about boys, for listening to every detail about my love life, and for giving thoughtful, expert advice on all things. And, of course, for flying across the country to celebrate this book with me! Your friendship means more to me than waffles.

TO MY SUPER SISTERS...

Thank you for a boundless supply of love, laughs, and dance parties. You help make the single life a little more "super." Gubby, I appreciate all of the delicious coffee beverages that you consistently provided me with throughout hours of editing, and Kash, for all the behind-the-scenes help you provided, I am so grateful. I love you both.

TO MY WONDERFUL GRAM...

Thank you for always taking such an avid interest in the events of my love life. You're the coolest grandmother in the world, hands down.

TO MY BELOVED GRANDFATHER...

Thank you for always believing in me and supporting me, no matter how grandiose of a dream I dreamt. I miss you every day.

TO POPPA B, MY STRONG, HANDSOME, AND SUPER COOL COUSIN...

I love our dinners where we gossip about the love lives of everyone in the family. Let's never stop doing that. Also, thank you for calling me "L-Money" and considering me to be a relationship expert.

TO AUNTIE SUZY AND UNCLE G...

Orange I glad that you're my godparents?? (I am.)

TO GRAM AND POPPY, AND AUNT LAURA AND UNCLE TOM...

Thank you for giving me outstanding examples of true love to aspire to – your magnificent love stores inspire me always.

TO MY LITTLE BAYBAY, DONNIE...

Thank you for the kisses, the (sometimes) snuggles, and for listening to me vent about boys.

AND FINALLY, TO ALL OF THE MEN IN THIS BOOK...

Thank you. Without you, I wouldn't have had a book to write.

Made in the USA
Middletown, DE
03 June 2016